Can, Sir!

With God's Help, I Can Do This!

Grace
PUBLISHING

COMPILED AND EDITED
BY YVONNE LEHMAN AND TERRI KALFAS

Scripture quotations marked CSB are taken from *The Christian Standard Bible*. Copyright © 2017 by Holman Bible Publishers. Used by permission. Christian Standard Bible®, and CSB® are federally registered trademarks of Holman Bible Publishers, all rights reserved.

Scripture quotations marked KJV are taken from the *King James Version* of the Bible.

Scripture quotations marked NASB are taken from the *New American Standard Bible*®, Copyright © 1960, 1971, 1977, 1995, 2020 by The Lockman Foundation. All rights reserved.

Scripture quotations marked NIV are taken from *The Holy Bible, New International Version*®, NIV® Copyright © 1973, 1978, 1984, 2011 by Biblica, Inc.® Used by permission. All rights reserved worldwide.

Scripture quotations marked NLT are taken from the *Holy Bible, New Living Translation*, copyright © 1996, 2004, 2015 by Tyndale House Foundation. Used by permission of Tyndale House Publishers, Inc., Carol Stream, Illinois 60188. All rights reserved.

Royalties for this book are donated to Samaritan's Purse.

CAN, SIR!
  WITH GOD'S HELP I CAN DO THIS!

ISBN-13: 978-1-60495-083-0

Copyright © 2022 by Grace Publishing House. Published in the USA by Grace Publishing House. All rights reserved. No part of this book may be reproduced in any form or by any electronic or mechanical means, including information storage and retrieval systems, without permission in writing, except as provided by USA Copyright law.

From Samaritan's Purse

We so appreciate your donating all royalties from the sale of the books *Divine Moments, Christmas Moments, Spoken Moments, Precious Precocious Moments, More Christmas Moments, Stupid Moments, Additional Christmas Moments, Loving Moments, Merry Christmas Moments, Cool-inary Moments, Moments with Billy Graham, Personal Titanic Moments, Remembering Christmas, Romantic Moments, Pandemic Moments, Christmas Stories, Broken Moments, Celebrating Christmas, Grandma's Cookie Jar* and now, *Can, Sir!* to Samaritan's Purse.

What a blessing that you would think of us! Thank you for your willingness to bless others and bring glory to God through your literary talents. Grace and peace to you.

Their Mission Statement:

Samaritan's Purse is a nondenominational evangelical Christian organization providing spiritual and physical aid to hurting people around the world.

Since 1970, Samaritan's Purse has helped victims of war, poverty, natural disasters, disease, and famine with the purpose of sharing God's love through his son, Jesus Christ.

Go and do likewise
Luke 10:37

You can learn more by visiting their website at
samaritanspurse.org

Dedicated to Yvonne Lehman,
who helped bring the Divine Moments series into being,

to the writers who share our vision,

and to the readers
we hope will be blessed by our stories.

CONTENTS

1. *Can't See* – Maureen Miller 7
2. *Dancing* – Beverly Varnado 10
3. *What a Moment, What a Day!* – Yvonne Lehman 14
4. *Peace Like a River* – Norma Mezoe 19
5. *At My Age? And a Pandemic Too!* – Ozlem Barnard 22
6. *Lifestyle Changes Beat Cancer* – Ginny Dean Brant 28
7. *When Joy Finally Comes* – Vicki H. Moss 33
8. *An Unlikely Source of Inspiration* – Ben Cooper 37
9. *The Temptation of Despair* – Mindy Gallagher 40
10. *Bad Hair Day* – Deb Gatz 42
11. *Riding a Roller Coaster in the Middle of a Storm* – Diana C. Derringer 45
12. *From Blindness to Greater Vision* – Beckie Horter 47
13. *Lee Has Cancer* – Rob Buck 50
14. *He Knows My Name* – Jeri McBryde 53
15. *Eighteen Days* – Bob Blundell 56
16. *Laughter from God* – Janet Ann Collins 59
17. *Intercession* – Steve Carter 60
18. *The Voice Within* – Lola Di Giulio De Maci 64

19. *My Faith Still Holds* – Diana Leagh Matthews 67

20. *The Green Envelope* – Tanja Dufrene 73

21. *The Last Chapter* – Brenda Miller 76

22. *Lessons Learned from Covid-19 Through the Cross* –
    Ginny Dean Brant 82

23. *A Hero's Hope* – Erma M. Ullrey 86

24. *The Challenges of Caregiving* – Norma C. Mezoe 90

25. *Through It All* – Diana C. Derringer 93

26. *Cancer and Chrysanthemums* – April Pope 94

27. *The Journey that Doesn't Make Sense* –
    Debbie Presnell 97

28. *The Enemy Within* – Marian Rizzo 101

29. *Embrace the Fleeting Days* –
    Ann Brubaker Greenleaf Wirtz 104

30. *What's My Number?* — Lydia E. Harris 108

31. *Laughing with God* – Esther M. Bailey 110

32. *Final Moments* – Barbara Ragsdale 113

33. *Three Little Words* – Nanette Snipes 115

34. *Thank You for Finding My Breast Cancer* –
    Melissa Henderson 117

35. *I Do* – Andrea Merrell 120

36. *The Breath of Life* – Yvonne Lehman 122

About The Authors 127

1

Can't See

Maureen Miller

*Now we see through a glass, darkly; but then face to face:
now I know in part; but then shall I know even as also I am known.*

1 Corinthians 13:12

Cancer seems to be everywhere, and although there aren't many things I can, in good conscience, say I truly hate, I honestly do feel as though I *hate* cancer. It causes fear. Pain. Death. It's a thief — ransacking lives. Robbing people of time. Stealing loved ones away too soon.

Some time ago I was trying to email a friend, inquiring about a mutual friend's father who'd been diagnosed with pancreatic cancer and was preparing for extensive and painful surgery. Even with all this, the doctors gave him a very slim chance for full recovery. As I typed my message, for some reason — when I tried to write the word *cancer* — my computer autocorrected and wrote instead, "Can see."

Can see?

I was struck and immediately thought, "No, I *Can't See*. I can't see why cancer has to be so prevalent. I can't see why so many good people leave so soon. I can't see why loved ones must be left behind to mourn in anguish.

I *Can't See!*

And it's true. I can't see why so many people are currently battling cancer. I pray for them. I hope for them. I want for them. More time. Less pain. More appetite. Less fear. More hair.

And for those closest to the ones battling cancer, I *can't see* how they endure — watching their loved ones suffer. Enduring, alongside their sick spouse, sleepless nights. Cries of agony. Whispers of dreams not yet realized. Hopeful prognoses turned to, "There's nothing more we can do. . . ." No —

I Can't See!

"Can see?" I scoffed. Stupid autocorrect. I typed slowly. Methodically. C-A-N-C-E-R. And when it finally appeared correctly, I moved on in my message.

But the real message — His message — is becoming more clear to me. And although I'll probably need to be reminded again (I'm a very slow and sometimes stubborn learner, after all!), the "take home" from this is just that —

I. Can't. See.

Not yet. I can't see any meaning in cancer. I can't see any meaning in pain. I can't see any meaning in loss. Because. . . .

I Can't See — because, for now, (I) only see through a glass darkly.

I can't see. . . .

No, of course not. My fleshly eyes only want to see that which is pleasant. I close them to things that are not. I want things my way. I'm a selfish person, after all. I forget that this world is not as it was intended. That selfishness such as mine (no better, no worse) tainted it long ago — is what stains it still.

Cancer, too — an ugly blemish upon an imperfect, sin-scarred world is not what God intended — no! But thankfully, through Christ, it's what He has, indeed, redeemed. I say it again, with thankfulness — and suddenly, the blinders of hate (even toward cancer) begin to fall away.

God, through Christ, has redeemed the world! Cancer doesn't get the last word. Pain and death don't either. Agony and loss aren't purposeless, as there's beauty in brokenness — purpose even in pain.

Ah, yes. Though there is much I, indeed, *cannot see* or fully understand just yet, perhaps through His lens of grace and with His enabling power, I *can see* some things. Maybe I can even *see* purpose in cancer — if such is, for some, the portal through which one must pass to enter his or her eternal home. And there, where pain and sickness are no more, one can finally see Jesus "face to face" (1 Corinthians 13:12b).

And even on this side of the veil, the light of His countenance does shine through — offering hope and lighting the way for all who seek Him, that we might see the path of peace and walk it. No matter the darkness — even the darkest night of one's soul. Yes, even cancer.

> *Dear Jesus, for all those who are facing cancer themselves or for those walking through its ugliness alongside another, we pray for your peace in the midst of this dark night of the soul. Merciful Savior, be ever near. Be ever present. Help us each to see as we walk in the light of your countenance, no matter what we each may face. Amen.*

2

Dancing

Beverly Varnado

"Postponed?" I cried into the phone.

"Yes," the nurse said, "we've experienced scheduling problems at the hospital and we've found it necessary to delay your surgery a week."

Another whole week of waiting. My breath left me. *I'll never make it.*

I hated waiting. All I wanted was to be done with this mastectomy and treatment. When would I get back to some kind of normal life?

"Is there not anything to be done?"

"I'm afraid not, this is the best we can do."

I sighed and clicked off the phone. I scanned my calendar lying on the table. I'd penciled in the family trip to Hilton Head Island, South Carolina, which we'd planned for months. With the original surgery date, I had planned to cancel the trip. We could go now, but it might be torture with my pretending to have fun while waiting for a mastectomy the day after we returned home. Could I pull this off with my husband, Jerry, eight-year-old son, Aaron, and seven-year-old daughter, Bethany, without making them miserable too?

I'd already waited a long time. In late April, a problem detected in my mammograms led to surgical biopsies in May on three areas in my right breast. The day I expected to get the biopsy results, I was told the information would need to be sent off to one of the leading experts in the world on atypical cells. That required more days of waiting. When the pathology report finally came back, it confirmed a cancer diagnosis.

Following the report, I waited to see a plastic surgeon, a radiologist, and an oncologist to get the information on my treatment options. When it finally seemed everything including the surgery date was decided, I got the phone call about changing the date. Feeling at the end of my rope, I didn't want to go on the family trip. I guess I just wanted to bathe in self-pity.

I called Jerry to tell him about the change in the surgery date.

"Oh, good," he said. "We can go on our vacation like we originally planned."

"I wonder if I'll be able to enjoy myself with this surgery waiting for me?"

"Sure, you will," my ever-optimistic husband said.

"If you say so," I mumbled, not sure at all.

We packed our things and our kids and headed off on what I hoped would not be a terrible mistake. My goal for the week was to avoid bursting into tears.

The first day we were there, I burst into tears. It seemed the tiniest little things made me cry — this time, the condition of the hotel room.

"The carpet's wet and the door lock is broken," I picked up my suitcase and carried it back out the door. "And the room looks dark."

Of course, the hotel gave us another room, but I didn't deal with the problem very well. It seemed a confirmation of what I predicted earlier.

Later, as I trekked to the swimming pool I sensed the Lord speaking to me. "Beverly, I have something special I want to do during this waiting time."

"Lord," I whispered, "please help me see the good you have for us here."

The second night Jerry wanted to use a gift certificate someone had given us to a nice restaurant on one of the inland waterways.

"Are you sure?" I asked. "I might cry again." I hated being that way.

"It'll be fine, even if you cry," Jerry encouraged. "Let's give it a try."

We walked into the restaurant to a woman's lovely, soulful singing. The waiter escorted us to a table right in front of the singer. As I ate my fresh shrimp, listened to the music, and gazed out on the blue waterway, a little sparkle of something I would call joy rose in me. After we finished eating, my husband took Bethany's hand and twirled her around on the dance floor. She threw her head back, laughing as she danced. They were a delight to behold.

I turned to Aaron and asked, "Will you dance with me?" He nodded, and our entire family was together, dancing and laughing.

The children sat as the singer crooned a slower song, and Jerry took me in his arms. I put my head on his shoulder. As we danced, tears rolled again, but they were not tears of sorrow, but of joy.

The next night, we were back along the inland waterway walking and talking. The voice of the same singer from the restaurant drifted toward us as she sang at another location. Jerry and I began to dance along the water's edge, under the stars as our children played nearby. It seemed we were dancing right in the face of cancer.

No one could ever take that moment from us.

When we left the island, I took that memory of dancing with me. The next few days were not easy ones. The surgery lasted four hours, then I suffered an adverse reaction to pain medication. I dealt with bandages and tubes and faced the possibility of chemotherapy.

Several days passed before the phone call finally came telling us the lymph nodes were clear. That meant no chemo.

Oh, how thankful we were!

Our wedding anniversary fell a week after my mastectomy.

"What can we do to celebrate?" I asked feeling awkward, so aware of my bandages and ugly drainage tubes, too encumbering for me to go out at that point.

"I have an idea," Jerry said.

He arranged for a friend to entertain our children at a pizzaria, then left and returned with deliciously-aromatic steaks from our favorite restaurant. We ate in the dining room, on good china, by soft candlelight.

Jerry looked at me across the table, "You're beautiful," he said with a dimpled smile, his eyes shining.

My eyes pooled with moisture. Again. "Thank you," I whispered.

After dinner he took out a CD we'd purchased of the singer during our pre-surgery vacation and put it in the player. Somehow, I secured the drainage tubes coming from my side. He held me in his arms, and we slow-danced, unhindered by bandages. As we danced, I remembered the twinkling stars and the blue water from the week before, and God's faithfulness to us in these days. God brought me safely through the surgery, and I didn't have to have chemotherapy.

On the trip I hadn't wanted to take, and during the waiting I dreaded, God answered my prayer and gave me one of the most amazing gifts I've ever received. He helped me reframe this entire period. He not only brought good out of the trip, but also gave me one of the sweetest memories I have in my life. When I think of mastectomy, I think of being held in my precious husband's arms, and I think of dancing.

At this writing, I am approaching my twentieth anniversary as a cancer survivor and I'm still dancing.

3
What a Moment, What a Day!

Yvonne Lehman

On September 11, 2001 my husband, Howard, and I watched TV in disbelief and horror as the World Trade Center was attacked and collapsed. We were getting ready to go to the doctor for what we considered a routine checkup because of Howard's itching and abdominal ache.

The topic of conversation at the doctor's office was the New York attack, despite the fact Howard and I were being sent to the hospital. The doctor suspected Howard had a gallstone or something wrong in the gallbladder. Testing took place for several days and the diagnosis came back that he had cancer of the bile duct and he needed to go to Duke for exploratory surgery.

For three weeks in October, while Howard lay in a hospital bed barely enduring numerous tests and ultimate surgery, we concentrated primarily on newspaper and TV reports of what was taking place in New York. After surgery, the doctor told us the cancer had spread too far on the liver, that half of the liver would have had to be removed, and that he couldn't chance that because of Howard's age and heart condition. Howard was eighty-one.

The doctor gave the diagnosis to Howard, me, and our four grown children: According to medical opinion Howard had six months, maximum, to live.

The diagnosis was as unacceptable to us as what had happened in New York. In the same way as the reality of NY began to penetrate our consciousness, so did this death sentence. Knowledge accompanied by disbelief, shock, and a kind of numbness. We know we're all going to die — someday — somehow —perhaps in the next moment — but never *this* moment.

The doctor, and all of us, believed in miracles.

Despite that, Howard's recuperation from surgery was questionable numerous times. When he was coherent, he insisted I sit on his bed and he planned for me to live a life without him. We'd "celebrated" our forty-third wedding anniversary at Duke, while he lay in a hospital bed. We'd never had a less active celebration, and at the same time, never a sweeter one. When one is faced with death, there is no concern about this rat race of a life we run. Nothing is more important than our love for each other and the realization that it is not life, but eternity that is ever present.

In spite of his physical suffering and knowing his time with family was limited, Howard faced death with assurance that he would be in heaven with the Lord Jesus. His concern was doing whatever the doctors thought best to improve or relieve pain while making me take notes on everything from his funeral, to life insurance, to how to change the filters in the fuel-oil furnace and where to buy windshield wiper fluid, something I'd never done in my life.

After returning home, Howard began his five weeks of daily radiation treatments, along with his chemo pack that needed changing once a week. By the time the treatment ended, he had to crawl into the house and I had to feed him numerous times, day and night, through a feeding tube. He lost thirty pounds.

His condition slowly improved for a couple of weeks and we were quite optimistic. After another examination however, the diagnosis came that he had only weeks to live. Hospice came, and their help was invaluable in every way as he went from a walker, to a wheel chair and eventually a hospital bed. As much as I regretted seeing that vital man deteriorate physically, and eventually mentally, I often thought of those who had lost loved ones so abruptly on September 11. I was blessed to have a time of preparation for this impending death. One is never totally prepared to lose a loved one, but acceptance of its inevitability helped me tremendously.

Did we get a miracle? Oh yes. It did not come in the manner of physical healing, although Howard lived nine months instead of six. We had many miracles. Our pastor/son brought his wife and family to stay with us for six weeks to help in any way. Another family member with small children came often. Two of my daughters, both nurses, stayed during the last two weeks of Howard's life and took over with his care. When he had to take medication every two hours, they wouldn't let me do anything.

We were able to keep Howard in his favorite recliner in the family room in front of the TV much of the time. We slept on the couch and the floor to be near him. We set up a card table and played scrabble, talked about all the wonderful times we'd spent together. When he couldn't talk, he indicated he could hear us. My two daughters and I bonded in a way we might never have under more pleasant circumstances. Children leave home at an early age, while parents are still viewed as unappreciated authority figures. During this time of Howard's illness, these daughters grew up. They matured into thoughtful, appreciative human beings concentrating on the important things in life, including inevitable death. They even learned to appreciate "Mom."

On June 17, I had been downstairs with one daughter while another, Cindy, sat beside Howard. I felt a great urge to go check on him.

"Do you notice a change in his breathing?" Cindy asked.

I walked in front of him. Yes, something was different. She hurriedly left the room. I sat beside him, put my arm across his chest to his shoulder, kissed his face and mouth and said, "I love you." He made a noise, for the first time in two days, and I knew he heard me and was responding, "I love you." No more breath came from him. I called the others. We sat around him and felt his warmth as long as it lasted.

Miracles during his illness, death, memorial service, and afterwards? Definitely! Friends, relatives, neighbors, church members, medical personnel, Hospice, and even people I didn't know sustained me with an outpouring of love, prayers, cards, calls, visits, food, food, food, and more food.

I consider it a miracle to have felt such tenderness and sweetness as my strong, vital husband became incapacitated. He came to need care like a newborn baby. I loved being able to care for him the way I had my babies. I thanked God I was able, that I was much younger than he and had the stamina to be helpful to him in his time of need.

Howard had always been quick to say he loved me. During this time, he told me many times a day that he loved and appreciated me. When he died, neither of us had anything left unsaid. We had no regrets. That brings peace that some don't have when faced with a loved one's sudden death.

God's peace is the most profound miracle. It truly does pass all understanding. It doesn't take away the feeling of loss. It didn't take away the physical exhaustion, nor the mental anguish. It doesn't take away the necessary process of grieving. But God's peace makes it all bearable.

Because of God and His Word, I can accept death as a part of life. I know we grow old. Disease and illness are rampant. We often face life with uncertainty, but I know we can face death and eternity with assurance.

After Howard's death, I was alone in a way I hadn't been in forty-three years. I missed Howard terribly. We were truly "two become one" in so many ways. After retirement from the Federal Prison System, he had his woodworking hobby and I had my writing ministry. We appreciated each other's abilities.

At his memorial service I felt sustained by the love and concern of others. Most of all, I felt sustained by God's peace.

The service on June 21, a week before Howard's eighty-second birthday, was beautiful. Our pastor of twenty years gave a beautiful eulogy. Our new pastor read scripture. Military honors were done, including the twenty-one-gun salute, and the USA flag presented to me. The crowning moment was when Promise Group (who sang at my writers conference) sang "What a Moment, What a Day," reminding us all that someday we will be reunited with our loved ones who are now in a better world.

Death steals our earthly lives away. But nothing can take away our memories, or what God has in store for those who accept his son as their personal Savior.

4
Peace Like a River

Norma Mezoe

*Peace I leave with you; my peace I give you.
I do not give to you as the world gives.
Do not let your hearts be troubled and do not be afraid.*

John 114:27 NIV

It had been a frustrating morning.

According to my husband, I could do nothing right. Much of the stress was directly related to his medical problems. Gene had Alzheimer's, a disease doctors have diagnosed as irreversible.

One of the side effects of the illness is an inability to reason and think things through. I tried to explain why something he wanted wasn't going to happen. He angrily accused me of not caring and of thinking only of myself. I heard those words many times whenever things did not go according to his wishes.

I needed to pick up our mail at the post office. I always keep a CD playing in the car, and as I turned the key in the ignition, a song played with words about promised peace — a peace as deep and wide as a river. I took a deep breath and allowed the words of the song to wash away the turmoil that threatened to chase away the peace only God can give.

Perhaps you are also a caregiver, and, at times, your load seems heavier than you can carry. You may suffer with a debilitating illness. Perhaps your finances are at an all-time low, and the mortgage payment will soon be due. Maybe your spouse is cheating on you and wants a divorce. Possibly, your child has become an addict and hope is dim that the need for help will be admitted or accepted.

Whatever the problem or heartache, God waits to give us His peace — a peace flowing like a tranquil river.

If you have never experienced God's enduring peace, open your heart to salvation in Jesus Christ today.

In My Valley
Norma C. Mezoe

In my valley, God placed a mountain.
He formed and molded it in His hands.
He knew in the loneliness of my valley
I needed a high place to stand.

In my sorrow, He offered contentment.
For my heartache he supplied sweet release.
He gave me forgiveness instead of resentment
And for turmoil a heart filled with peace.

Yes, in my valley God placed a mountain
In the middle of my valley of pain.
He created a life-giving fountain
And shelter from life's threatening rain.

Over the mountain, God placed a rainbow
And set it in a background of blue.
Then He reminded me when my head is bowed low
To remember He always is true.

My Anchor Holds
Norma C. Mezoe

The tree, stripped of
its leafy clothing, is
all bare twigs and branches.
A lone bird nest struggles to
hold to its anchor as
the wind blows wildly.

At times I identify
with that naked tree . . .
My soul stripped down to
its bare bones as another storm
blows through my life.
Like the bird nest, I struggle
to hold to my Anchor.

And I thank my God
that when my strength is gone,
when I cannot hold on,
He will hold on to me.

5

At My Age?
And a Pandemic Too!

Ozlem Barnard

As I get older, fear wants to wrap itself around me more. Sometimes I invite it into my life with my *what-ifs*. Other times it comes uninvited. This time around, fear, induced by my pregnancy in mature age and intensified in the coronavirus era, came to me uninvited, but I committed the error of embellishing my fear with my *what-ifs*. I had to do something to get out of fear's embrace, and I decided to learn to trust God.

In January, I had spent a day at a beach in Los Angeles, soaking up the sun — a rarity in the often-cloudy D.C. in winter. I had grown up looking out at sun-swept beaches, and I felt nostalgic for the blue vistas of my youth. Looking out over the calm, turquoise water from my hotel room, I pondered how I wanted to spend the second half of my life (and why couldn't I live in sunny California?).

I had noticed that I had missed my period a few weeks before. In the swirl of my busy life, I had not paid the issue much mind. Earlier in the day, I had even joked with my friend, "I am either going through menopause or I am pregnant." At forty-four, unaware of God's big surprise for me, I was sure that menopause was the more realistic possibility.

Upon returning to D.C. everything annoyed me: the winter weather, the lack of sun, the lack of any beaches nearby, my never-ending commute, long work hours, the lack of free time, dissatisfaction with the hundred small problems with my house. Even though, in retrospect, none of these frustrations were all that important, I felt a mounting stress. A high level of low emotions was cycling through my body. *This mid-life thing was going to be tougher than I thought.*

Deep in my soul, I had not taken the idea of possibly being pregnant seriously, though intellectually I understood that I could not completely discount it. I had read that the chance of getting pregnant at my age was less than two percent, but I had to rule it out. Besides setting my mind at ease, it would also allow me to be able to drink some wine guilt-free while holding a pity-party for my early menopausal self.

Since the birth of my second son eleven years earlier, my husband has passionately desired to have one more child. While I loved children, and we had tried a few times to conceive, in my heart I had always been on the fence because of my many nagging fears and worries. *What if I have another (third) boy? What if the baby is not healthy? What if I feel claustrophobic and have panic attacks again during pregnancy? What-if another baby hinders my career development?*

I had let my fears rule my decisions as the years stretched out after the birth of my second child. Time eventually seemed to stretch too far, and I feared that the window of new motherhood was closing. By the time I turned forty, with the pangs of regret, I experienced a new fear: that the baby train had left my station forever.

Nevertheless, feeling a bit foolish at my age I dutifully purchased a pregnancy test.

My mind was not on the test itself, but rather was running through the memories of all the other times I had seen negative results over the years. Caught up in a somewhat melancholy reverie, I glanced at these results.

Wait! What? Pregnant? My heart raced with joy and fear. Simultaneously, I was over the top of the clouds and deep under the ground; ecstatic and terrified; hopeful and fearful. All day I could barely wait to tell my husband. Unable to wait any longer, I called him at work, asking him to come pick me up, but not explaining why I needed to see him so urgently.

We walked in a cold winter wind among the bare D.C. cherry trees. When I finally gave him the news, he was very happy, though slightly dazed with shock. It was not what he expected to hear that day. We were, of course, thankful, but were unable to fully process this little miracle God was giving us. Normally an annoyingly and relentlessly optimistic man, my husband surprised me when he said, fearfully, "Honey, remember the high risk of miscarriage at our age." He was trying to protect me from heartbreak, but I did not want to hear any new fears. Driving home, we were speechless. *Was it real? Will it last?*

Over the ensuing weeks, I wrestled with my fears of the unknown. My feelings formed a triangle of happiness, embarrassment, and worry. I smiled when I thought of a baby in my arms. I could almost smell that heavenly baby smell. But whenever I caught of a glimpse of my graying hair, an embarrassment captured me. *Who did I think I was being pregnant at this age?*

The Internet certainly did not help. Everything I read warned about my age's high miscarriage rate and the other risks related to mature-age pregnancy. Eventually, I stopped searching for information, because it only helped reinforce my growing sense of worry. I feared that if I took a wrong step my uterus would shatter into little pieces, as if it was made of glass.

We went to the doctor to confirm the over-the-counter test. Doctors, with their training and experience, can be both reassuring and terrifying. "What causes miscarriage is not necessarily something you do," my doctor told me. She informed me that many factors cause miscarriage, and almost all were out of my control. Moreover, even if the baby survived the first trimester, statistics showed that risks of health issues — for both me baby and me — were high at my age.

While I struggled with my fears about the pregnancy, the whole world came to a halt as we all learned a new fear: the coronavirus. In

January and February of 2020, we knew that virus existed, but it seemed like a faraway danger until it suddenly arrived in the middle of our lives in March. Like so many others, our family went into full lockdown. The isolation and constant drumbeat of fearful stories in the news was terrifying; but at least we had the comfort of being isolated together. The first couple of months during the lockdown, I was ultra-anxious to protect my family — including and especially my unborn daughter — against this unseen enemy. No measure was good enough. I read the news constantly and barked orders at my family: Wash your hands. Clean the groceries. Sanitize the delivery boxes before taking them in.

I struggled with coming to terms with these matters outside of my control. But I also knew that no amount of worrying could fix my problems. After all I could not add a single hour to my life (or my family members' lives) by worrying. (Luke 12:22.) To tackle my fears, after much consideration and praying, I decided to do what was within my power and to trust God with the rest.

To do that, I needed to push away my *what-if* fears. If I'd let my *what-if* fears run free, even Shakespeare's Hamlet would have looked pale in comparison to the fake theater playing in my head. A bit of wisdom I have gained over forty-four years helped me recognize when I am embellishing a risk in my head. I've learned that I must talk back to my fears, refusing to let them dominate my thinking. I've also learned that I must defy my yearning for certainty. After all, almost nothing is certain in life. When I cannot even guarantee my next breath, expecting to control the outcome of every situation seems ridiculous.

Something that helped me was the recognition that we, as a society, normalize many situations in our daily life even though they contain high risks. For instance, I dread the day my oldest son will start driving, but I wouldn't think of preventing him from getting his license.

When things get more novel, however, my fear of the unknown takes over. I had been fearful in my first two pregnancies, but it was new to fear that my age was presenting new risks or that a global pandemic could put the pregnancy in danger. While certainly nerve-wracking, I could not just let these novel anxieties paralyze me.

I decided to stop being a passive worrier and to try instead to be an action-taker.

I cannot guarantee that my unborn baby will never have a health issue, but I can give her the best possible chance by praying and listening to the medical professionals God has placed in my path. I cannot make coronavirus disappear or protect my family from it one hundred percent, but I can take reasonable measures to decrease the risks of my family getting the virus, while also giving them the space to live and thrive as best we can in this strange era.

When I take things one day at a time and focus on what I can do, and don't dwell on what I cannot control, I produce fewer *what-if* fears and find it easier to overcome my anxiety. I focus instead on the present. I pray. I study the Bible. I exercise and take walks with my loved ones. I eat healthy foods. I try to get enough sleep. I spend quality, loving time with my family. Filling my days with these actions helps me manage my fears productively.

I also try to trust God more, knowing that He will take care of things outside of my control. I try to cast away my fears to God. But trusting God with all my worries, all the time, is challenging, because I like being in charge of my situation. Despite my efforts, the fears work their way back into my heart. If I focus on these fears, I would make myself miserable every minute of the day.

Surrendering control — to include giving up my fears — is not easy but I know that this is His path. I have dwelt on the mountain of fear so long, I recognize that it is time to come down to the valley of peace that God is promising me. As I mature in my faith and daily practice trusting God more, I know I will get better at not taking my worries back from Him.

For now, I am finding peace in His words while learning to trust

Him. He tells me not to worry about tomorrow (Matthew 6:25) and to put my trust in Him when I am afraid (Psalm 56:3). That is what I now try to practice, one day at a time.

Sadly, we are not planning to move to sunny California any time soon. But the little seed of hope God planted inside me warms my heart. There will be new fears and worries that will try to get a hold in my heart. But I know that through trust in God everything will be all right.

6
Lifestyle Changes Beat Cancer

Ginny Dent Brant

Three strikes drove me to my knees.

Strike 1. "You have cancer."

Strike 2. "It's aggressive."

Strike 3. "It appears the cancer has spread."

That shook me to the core. Three strikes! Am I'm out? And what about my healthy lifestyle?

The news of a cancer diagnosis has a profound impact on the body and immune system. In desperation, I made an appointment to see the chaplain at Cancer Treatment Centers of America.

As I sobbed uncontrollably, Chaplain Eric Sewell gently held my hand. I had questions. I needed answers. I started with my real concerns, "Would all these treatments leave me disabled and negatively affect my quality of life?"

I explained that the last fifteen years of my life had been centered on helping care for my parents and in-laws until their deaths while managing a full time job. Watching them decline into disability was devastating to me. My emotions were still raw from my mother's passing.

"I understand your fears of being disabled," he responded. "Chemotherapy is a doable thing. Your medical records show that you are healthy with no complicating factors."

"But if I'm so healthy, why did I get cancer?" I asked.

"Sometimes the why is hard to know, but I do know this: Patients who are healthy, have positive attitudes, and rely on their faith do much better than those who don't. If you're overweight, or suffering from diabetes, high blood pressure, and other problems, your body will have more problems with the chemo."

"Really? So my good health habits that did not prevent my cancer will help me survive chemo?"

"Yes," he replied.

That led me to my final question, "How could a health nut like me end up with an aggressive cancer like this?"

"Ginny, consider it a gift from God. Sometimes God allows things in your life for you to help others. As an author and speaker, your experience in this journey can be a guiding light to others."

"But it's the gift I never wanted." I blurted remembering I'd said this for the third time. The Apostle Paul prayed three times for his thorn to be removed. And I was praying this cancer thorn would disappear.

"Yes, I can see it now — your next book with this inscription — *the book I never wanted to write*," he chuckled. "In time, you will see the hand of God."

After leaving his office, I examined my lifestyle habits. Was I really a health nut? Which ones do I need to improve? Which lifestyle habits would help me survive all these treatments? I knew that daily prayer must increase during this arduous journey. I needed its supernatural power.

I considered the nutrient God created on the first day — water. Hydration is directly connected to health. Every system in our body must have sufficient water to work properly. Jesus compared our need of Him to our bodies' need for water.

I set up a plan to hydrate my body with an increase in water before, during, and after chemotherapy as my nutritionist recommended. This meticulous attention to hydration enabled my chemo to work properly and also removed the toxic residue from my body afterwards.

Then I looked at exercise. I was already exercising by walking several times each week. Instinctively, I began including exercise in every aspect of my treatment.

Exercise played a key role in my recovery following numerous surgeries. After my first surgery, I had multiple tubes protruding from my body.

"When can these tubes be removed?" I asked.

"The catheter can be removed by tomorrow morning, if you are able to walk four rounds of this floor," the nurse responded.

"Let's go." I told the nurse the following morning.

I completed one lap. It felt good to move. I did another lap. Then a third, fourth, etc.

"How many to a mile?" I asked.

"Eighteen — but you can't do that!"

"Don't say can't," I challenged.

This cancer was trying to beat me. I was fighting back. While I continued the laps, the nurse consulted with my surgeon.

"It's okay," my surgeon said. "If she has the energy and balance, it will only work for her good."

The nurses were cheering me on as I rounded the 1eighteenth lap. I felt like Dale Earnhardt, Jr.

"Hooray," they applauded. But I kept on going.

Then I hit mile marker two. I felt like Forest Gump when he finished his run across America.

My respiratory therapist encouraged, "Good for you. Exercise oxygenates your body and lungs. You promoted your own healing."

Catheter removed. But walking also helped kick-started my organs, pumped anesthesia out of my body, relieved stress, lessened the threat of blood clots, sped up the draining of my breast tissue, and lifted my spirits.

I received an added benefit when my surgeon released me. I went home without any attached drainage tubes. That's a victory in Jesus for a breast cancer patient!

Exercise also benefitted me with the Big Bad Wolf of my journey — chemotherapy. I made it a goal to walk one to two miles before and after each infusion. After chemotherapy, exercise along with hydration stimulates the lymphatic system to remove the trash from our cells. Our lymphatic system is a part of our immune system and requires us to move as it gathers and removes toxins from our bodies.

An oncologist, Dr. Jeffrey Guiguere, was shocked when I was able to walk two miles the day after my fourth chemotherapy infusion. "Your movement is serving you well," he said. "I wish more of my patients would do the same."

Your bowels must keep moving after chemotherapy. If your colon does not move those toxins out of your body in a timely manner, they can be reabsorbed into your system.

My movement also actually helped my chemotherapy to target my cancer. When you are undergoing chemotherapy, you want your body working at optimum levels. In this way, you are helping your doctor to increase your chances of survival.

The aromatase inhibitor pill or estrogen-blockers given to many breast cancer patients continue their treatments for five to ten years. The side effects include loss of bone density, depression, joint pain, brain fog, and insomnia. As a result, many women depend on medications to compensate. Exercise helped me relieve all these symptoms.

Years ago, cancer patients were told to stay in bed and limit physical movement. No more! The Clinical Oncology Society of Australia's (COSA) position after multitudes of research on exercise and cancer now recommends that exercise be a part of every patient's cancer treatment plan, used to counteract the adverse effects of treatments. This news has sent shockwaves throughout the cancer treatment world.

Doctors now know that exercise boosts the immune function, increases oxygen and nutrients to the cells and brain, reduces insulin levels, reduces stress, increases mitochondria, and causes you to sweat out toxins.

When one is in a cancer journey, physical exercise is not to be ignored just because you don't feel well. Dr. Kenna Barber called me a "Rock Star" cancer patient when my red and white blood cells were back within normal limits just six weeks after my last chemotherapy. This usually takes up to five years.

What about the impact of sleep in the cancer journey? It's the single most important activity we do in life, and it comprises one third of our day. Seven to nine hours is recommended and like exercise, it's free!

Our bodies repair and defend against cancer when we are in deep sleep. While we are snoozing, our body improves brain function, reduces cortisol and stress levels, repairs our bodies, fights cancer, and recharges our energy levels. However, according to Dr. Russell Foster, long-term sleep deprivation can lead to a suppressed immune system, increasing our chances for infection, cancer, and cardiovascular disease.

Dr. Daniel Amen says, "Our brain washes and cleans itself while we are sleeping."

By making sleep a priority, I was helping my body to beat cancer.

Although I had viewed myself as eating a healthy diet before cancer, I had more to learn about the healing chemicals God has provided for us in fruits and vegetables. I increased my fruits and vegetables from six daily to thirteen — eating more vegetables than fruits and selecting organic. These precious gifts of nature contain polyphenols, phytochemicals, antioxidants, fiber, vitamins, and minerals.

Junk foods and processed foods help cause cancer while whole foods help beat cancer.

In my cancer journey, I learned my body was designed to heal itself. But I must acquire the right lifestyle habits to help my body heal.

The best cure is you. Be your own best advocate by properly hydrating, moving throughout your cancer journey, getting restorative sleep, and eating the foods God has given us in nature. These lifestyle habits help your body heal, survive the treatments, and send signals to you brain encouraging your body to live. And fervent prayer gives you the power to make these changes.

Yes, lifestyle changes do beat cancer!

7
When Joy Finally Comes

Vicki H. Moss

"The tumor on his lung is the size of my fist," Dad's internist said, holding his fist up to the X-ray. "See that dark spot there. He has four months to live."

I heard the Holy Spirit's soft whisper, "Three months."

Thanking the doctor, I turned to leave. The bad news would be delivered later to the patient.

I almost worried myself to death during the next hours. I knew Daddy wouldn't want to go to a nursing home. He'd always planned to stay in his home until the bitter end. And he'd always been terrified of hospitals. The smell of hospitals terrified him as well. I knew the upcoming months would be long and hard. The time to tell him finally arrived.

"Who says I'm dying?" Daddy demanded.

Confused, I replied, "Your doctor. He showed me the X-ray. You have a tumor on one lung the size of your fist. Daddy, I just want you to know, I'll try my best to take good care of you." Speaking while wiping away spilling tears, I added, "When the cancer progresses, Hospice will come to the house when needed. You won't be alone. You'll be taken care of."

The next days were difficult. Daddy vacillated about his imminent death. One minute he couldn't believe he was dying. The next minute he was down in his coffee dregs. We'd already planned his funeral years earlier. I'd helped him choose the songs that would be sung during the service. I promised he'd have the same kind of funeral he'd given

Mother — down to the vault she was buried in, that was guaranteed not to leak. He was as prepared as anyone could be, considering death wasn't a lovely thing to think about, and one could never be totally reconciled with leaving this world and precious family behind.

When he finally came to grips with the fact that cancer was getting the best of him, there was one thing he couldn't shake: the pain in his back that wouldn't go away. He eventually asked for the prescribed pain pills.

The days consisted of watching movies. Nonstop war movies. *A Bridge Too Far* was one of his favorites. I helped him fight WWII all over again. He'd been in the first wave of boats to cross the Rhine, with machine gun fire mowing down everyone in his boat but him and one other. *Heaven Knows, Mister Alison,* starring Robert Mitchum, was another war movie that I loved as well. When I wasn't singing along with Robert Mitchum, "Don't sit under the apple tree with anyone else but me," I cooked Dad's favorite meals.

He requested salmon patties the way Mother had prepared them. Fried okra and squash were other favorite foods. One day, he asked for cornbread crumbled into a glass of milk — a treat he'd always loved. Every day he wanted ice cream. He got it. Boat loads. And every day he wanted his pain pills. I doled his meds out too, until the hospice nurse said go slow on the medication because the pain might get worse during his final days and they wouldn't work if his body craved more than the pills could deliver. So, Daddy went cold turkey on the pain pills altogether.

Then one day, I heard the old soldier say, "I'm tired of fighting that war. Can you fix me a soft egg?"

So with soft scrambled eggs, we watched *Gone with the Wind.* Over. And over. The movie was Mother's favorite. Perhaps he was preparing himself to see her again, real soon.

The pastor came to visit one day and asked me for a few private moments alone. I knew he was going to ask Daddy if he'd made his peace with his Lord. I'd already asked. And Daddy said, "Yes. I'm sure of my salvation. I believe Jesus died for my sins." But I let the pastor have his time anyway while I walked the road to the barn. Standing there next to the hot wire, I looked out at the cattle watching me. I began singing "Amazing Grace." They came, one by one. And stood before me in a row. Like they knew what was happening back there in the house. Like they were grieving with me. Or at least showing respect. That's what I pretended to believe anyway. In reality, however, they were only curious youngsters watching a human who lived in a foggy haze during those long hard days and nights.

Finally, back in the house, and with the pastor out of earshot, Daddy said, "Why did you stay outside so long?" He was fearful of being left alone, especially with people he wasn't familiar with.

How could I say, "I needed a break from the sadness."

"I'm here Daddy," I replied. "I'm here now."

The time came for a hospital bed to be brought in, along with a GEO-mattress to help prevent bedsores. Not long after, solid food was no longer needed. Ensure had taken its place for Daddy's only food source. Shortly after the last container of Ensure, Daddy went into a coma with only his breathing noticeable, letting me know he was partly alive. I thought about Robert Mitchum dying of lung cancer. I thought of a couple of things that Mitchum and Daddy had in common: Cigarette smoking and lung cancer.

That night, with Jasper, my Yorkie dog, settled on the reclining chair next to me, I heard my fur baby yelp. Strange. I'd never heard him yelp like that before. He usually whined when he needed to go outside. But I took him out. Looking up at the sky, I noticed how dark the night was. Inky black. And I knew it wouldn't be long until Daddy was being escorted to heaven.

"Jasper," I said, "you're not even serious about doing anything. Hurry up so we can go back inside. It's freezing out here." Nothing. Jasper sniffed around, doing everything but what he was supposed to be doing. "That's it buddy. Rattlesnakes out here can swallow you whole.

And they've been known to stick their heads out in winter. We're headed back to bed."

Back inside the great room, I settled in the recliner with Jasper next to me. I heard the sounds of the GEO mattress a foot from me but I no longer heard the labored breathing of my father. Suddenly, it dawned on me that Daddy had already passed away. Jasper's previous yelp was one of fright as he must have witnessed or sensed the angels taking Daddy before him.

And just like that, Daddy had been whisked away in spirit three months after his cancer diagnosis. His earthly days of fighting were over. I left my recliner and reached for Daddy's wrist to check his pulse. Then I checked his legs, just as Hospice had instructed. All of the splotchy purple signs of death were there. Indeed he was gone. But what should have been a time for rejoicing was a time of sadness. Only after Hospice arrived did the floodgates of weeping finally open. What I had wanted to be a time of rejoicing over what he had gained, was a time of great sadness over what I had lost.

Weeks later, still missing my father, I stood beneath his apple trees and watched the cattle in the pasture. I couldn't help but softly sing, "Don't sit under the apple trees with anyone else but me. . . ." I couldn't stop thinking about him. One night, he visited me in a dream. I said, "Daddy, is heaven all you thought it would be? Are you happy now?" He replied, "Yes." Then he was gone.

When morning came and I remembered the dream, I also recalled the verse in Psalm 30:5: *Weeping may tarry for the night, but joy comes with the morning.*

And now, more than ever, I know those words to be true.

8
An Unlikely Source of Inspiration

Ben Cooper

"You have cancer" are the worse three words you ever want to hear a doctor say. Your heart drops to your stomach and you don't even know how to react because you are numbed by the prognosis. The brain takes time to process all that those three words mean.

I should know, I've heard those words twice within a fifteen-year time frame. It truly is a tough pill to swallow, and the second time around does not make it any easier.

The first diagnosis came just after the birth of my youngest child. I was a husband, father of five, and thinking that should be the best time of life. The cries came, "Why me? Why can't some heinous murderer on death row have this instead of me?"

And then, the reflective reply, "Why not me? Who am I that I should get a pass? What makes me so special to think I would be exempt?" The sad reality is, cancer is not a discriminator and even prisoners on death row get it.

So, how do you get into the best place in your head to meet this challenge? My Christian faith tells me that prayer is the best place to start. After a short time, I began to see the cancer as a way to reaffirm my life, and to let it make me more acutely aware of what is meaningful and important. Then I wasn't consumed with cancer and thoughts of whether I would make it through surgery and the follow up treatments. My mind was reset to be thankful that I had cancer.

Wait! How on God's green earth can someone in their right mind even think of being thankful after receiving one cancer diagnosis, let alone two? Well, let me explain.

I was thankful that *I* — not my wife or any of my five children — had cancer. My mental therapy was that God saw fit to permit "Me" to have cancer so that my wife or children didn't have to go through it. Cancer helped me realize how hard it is for those who can't transfer it onto themselves for the sake of their loved ones.

In both cases, my level of coming out of this successfully was a conjured-up percentage by some set of medical statistics that really didn't mean a hill of beans to me. Because I was thankful that it was me dealing with the issue, I went into the first surgery after having one of the most peaceful night's sleeps I can ever remember without using any medications. And that comes from knowing that I might never wake up or be the same once that ten-and-a-half-hour surgery began.

All I had to do during surgery and treatments that followed was to lie down. I was prepared as well as I could be without any guarantees of the outcome. God saw fit to allow my life on this planet to continue as a husband, a father, and a testament that finding out what really matters in life can come from something as dark and ugly as cancer.

When the second diagnosis came twelve years later, it still took me by surprise. For two days, I worried and fretted and was consumed with the idea of going through all of it again. But on day three, I remembered that God had laid it on my heart to write a book. That had been long before the first cancer diagnosis. So, I traded worry for paper and ink and began to refocus my mind on writing. It became therapy for me.

The three months of waiting between diagnosis and surgery can be an eternity. I wrote, and when surgery day came, I got through it and went back home to continue to write. My book was published and has done quite well. Could it be that I had to get cancer the second time to motivate me to write that book? Anything is possible with God in control.

If I had the power to pick life with cancer or without cancer, I would choose "with" every time. It showed me the meaning of life from a very unexpected place. I truly have an inspired life.

9
The Temptation of Despair

By Mindy Gallagher

I don't know that I like living this long.
Long enough to stand by and watch my grown children
make big messes of the lives I birthed them to enjoy.
Long enough to learn new medical terminology
like a lobulated mass.
Long enough to watch my husband find words out of his grasp
that were once easily accessible.

When I had only lived a short time,
I was unfamiliar with such stresses.
I didn't bury close friends.
I didn't take anxiety medication.

Living this long is no picnic.

Although,
I am done striving to run the race
with my father's voice in my head chanting
work harder, climb higher, reach the top.
And true,
I can enjoy the peace of a warm afternoon
with nothing on my agenda;
exploring new areas of learning,
discovering the thrill of reinventing myself.

Still, these simple pleasures come at a high price.

Age.
And the stunning revelation that we are mortal.
Whether it happens tomorrow or years from now,
each one of us is destined to leave this earth.
We've been on that journey since we were born —
we just didn't often stop to think about it.
Now we can't help but acknowledge it,
as it constantly shows its ugly face
and shocks us awake
just when we've been lulled
into a false sense of immortality.

I don't think I like living this long,
and yet I don't think I like the alternative.

So, I pray for negative CT scan results.
I weep with grieving friends.
I muster great courage to be cheerful in the midst of uncertainty,
and grow closer to God through all that He adds to my plate.

Above all, I strive to see beauty in the midst of ugliness;
hope in the heartache, and joy in the sorrow —
these medicines that continue to heal
and without which I would most certainly
yield to the temptation of despair.
And so, today I am thankful:
For healthy children who are making their way
in fits and starts through this life;
A best friend whose cancer was recently declared in remission;
Moments my husband does not need to be reminded of something,
And,
a life lived long enough to understand
the immeasurable power of a grateful heart.

10

Bad Hair Day

Deb Gatz

You might find one here or there — an annoyance you just flick into the trash or pull off a coat and toss out the car window. I saw one a month or more ago, and renewed the routine of my past by picking it up and throwing it into the trash can by my bed. Then suddenly I picked up the trashcan and searched frantically, trying to find it. Where had it gone? It looked to be about one to two inches long and was the first one I had seen that was long enough to notice in almost a year!

A hair.

One slender, short, solitary reminder of what I — and my entire family — had been through for the past year. My hands were cautiously digging around in the trashcan in order to hold it, measure it, and even just stare at it for a little while. I longed to hold it in the palm of my hand, to feel the tickle and miniscule weight of it — and to stare at its promise.

It promised that things were swinging back to normal.

There were still doctors' visits, lots of them. There was still bone pain. There were still visits to the hospital for blood tests, scans, and more infusions, radiation, and surgeries. There was a lot of ground to re-gain that had been lost — energy and strength being chief among them. There were still concerns with every new ache and pain or perceived lump that was discovered. But the draining days with chemotherapy were over at least. The loss of appetite, feelings of nausea, thrush (yuck!), absence of strength, shortness of temper due to steroids . . . all of those things were improving.

And each one was evidenced by that short little hair.

We put a lot of stock in hair, don't we? Between shampoos, products, cuts, styles, coloring, etc., having hair can come at quite a price. Between February of 2009 and April of 2010, I needed only three haircuts. That's not counting the shave I had following the start of chemo that left me looking like a porcupine and wondering how on earth guys with hair one-quarter of an inch long can stand how it feels. Shortly after that shave, I found a new use for my lint roller. I used it to take care of all the little leftover hairs that were falling out every day. It worked great!

But that was after the first time, when masses of hair began falling out in my brush and hands. The first day it happened I admit, I was angry and sad all at the same time. I cried and cried. How on earth does one have crying jags without their family seeing, so they don't hurt, too? How does a person tell God it just isn't fair when, in reality, we know He is crying right there with us, holding us through it? How do people enter something like this without a family beside them? I'm so glad for both my biological family and my church family that have meant the world to me.

But, honestly, it's just hair. I can say that now. Put in perspective, there are things much worse to lose than hair.

We could lose our sanity. How many moms with little children have felt that way? We could lose our homes to a fire so that years of memories go up in smoke. We could lose a loved one. This past year at church has been so hard with the passing of those we have known and loved. We could lose our credibility or integrity. But I think more than any of those very hard, very difficult things, the worst things we can lose are opportunities — opportunities to see what God has for us — by choosing instead to walk right past them.

Only each individual knows what opportunities the Lord has put in his or her life. Opportunities to love others as God loves us, to show Him our love through service and obedience. Opportunities to diligently raise our children to honor Him; to love our spouse — especially in the hard times — and keep our eyes off the grass that often looks greener.

Opportunities to speak or live the Gospel out loud, when we know the Spirit of God is prodding us to just say it. Opportunities to be honest, but to speak the truth in love, knowing that it's just as possible for us to fail as it is for someone else.

But most of all, what if you have walked past the opportunity to accept the most astounding gift ever offered humanity? It's the gift of eternal life through the death and resurrection of Jesus Christ on your behalf?

I invite you to investigate for yourself the claims of Christ. Be honest with your questions and be willing to accept the answers that are found in the Bible.

None of us want to be called upon to pay the price for all the things we do that will separate us from Jesus forever. Sin is costly, but we can trust that Jesus paid the price for us. The Bible tells us *when we were utterly helpless, Christ came at just the right time and died for us sinners* (Romans 5:6 NLT). At just the right time, He paid the price for our sin so we don't have to pay it. At just the right time, He gives us the opportunity to admit that we need Him, accept His gift to put the past behind us, and turn a new page in our lives. He loves every person that much — to give us the opportunity of a lifetime.

And I can guarantee you . . . it's better than having hair!

11

Riding a Roller Coaster in the Middle of a Storm

Diana C. Derringer

He got up, rebuked the wind and said to the waves, "Quiet! Be still!" Then the wind died down and it was completely calm.

Mark 4:39 NIV

"It was the best of times. It was the worst of times." So begins Charles Dickens' *A Tale of Two Cities*. My husband and I can say the same about the past eighteen years. After hearing words like "brain tumor," "cancer," and "stage III anaplastic astrocytoma," our lives changed forever. For months we rode an emotional roller coaster.

When we learned my husband had a brain tumor, initial tests indicated it was probably nonmalignant. We clung to that hope.

The tumor, however, could not be removed without devastating damage to speech and memory. In addition, a surgical biopsy proved the mass was both malignant and aggressive, a grim diagnosis. Hope plummeted, as we prepared for his lengthy and intensive treatment process.

Minutes before our departure time for pre-radiation measurements, the telephone rang. A recent CT scan showed no evidence of a tumor. Hope soared as we notified friends and family.

A few days later, a follow-up MRI to verify the tumor's absence, gave disappointing results. Emotions nose-dived again.

My husband rarely sheds a tear. I cry at the drop of a hat. Shortly after his diagnosis, we shared one good cry. With that emotional release we felt better prepared to handle what lay ahead. Yet, in a greater sense, we haven't handled this situation. We've leaned on the strength God provides, daily trusting that God will see us through.

After three and one-half years we rejoiced in the news of remission. No chemotherapy capsules five nights each month. No medication to prevent nausea. Increased energy, appetite, and sleep.

At the same time, MRI's, blood tests, and numerous medical appointments became our new normal.

Has this been hard? Definitely. Do we understand all about it? No. Do we have any guarantees for the future? Of course not! No one does.

Nevertheless, in the midst of this ordeal, God blessed us in ways we would never have known otherwise. We experienced peace, joy, and comfort beyond words and an appreciation for the beauty and opportunities of each day. When physically and emotionally spent, God lifted us and gave exactly what we needed for that day.

We also received unbelievable support from family, friends, my husband's former employer, and our church. Their love and concern overwhelmed us at times. Relationships grew deeper and more meaningful.

If we're riding a roller coaster and a storm pops up, we have no choice but to complete the ride. Fellow passengers may scream or tremble. Others may gripe about those in control. A few may gaze in awe at the magnificent natural strength and beauty displayed.

Likewise, we have no choice about a number of life's circumstances, but we always have a choice in our reaction. Will we shrink in terror, crumble in despair, strike out in anger, and remain stuck in those emotions? Or will we learn to experience them and then let them go. Will we make the most of this fearsome yet exhilarating ride?

If we ask God for His peace, He will carry us through all of life's storms.

12

From Blindness to Greater Vision

Beckie Horter

Twenty years ago, my life changed radically. The diagnosis of a blinding retinal disease put a stop to life as I knew it. Plans for the future got iced. I grappled with the impossible realization that over time my central vision would be erased bit by bit. First in one eye, then the other. My condition would progress slowly, but predictably, and always with the threat of total blindness.

I was thirty-three years old.

As I struggled to come to terms with vision loss, practical matters took precedence. Obviously I could no longer continue my job proofreading the newspaper; the pace was too hectic. I stopped driving a car, and ouch! That hurt. Daily matters like reading my mail and quick stops at the grocery store became arduous tasks.

About that time, my sister hosted a birthday party for my mother. I looked across the room where my big family was gathered, and I couldn't tell who was who. I felt sick as I contemplated my blurry future.

I started to wonder . . . *Why had God allowed this to happen? Was I being punished? What type of future could I have as a legally blind person?*

The grieving process set in. From denial to bargaining, anger to depression, and then back again, my emotions ricocheted. Peace eluded me. The final step — acceptance — came after much wrestling with God.

One morning as I searched the Scriptures for answers, I read Psalm 34:18 (NIV): *The Lord is close to the brokenhearted and saves those who are crushed in spirit."*

The verse leapt off the page! Surely this was written just for me. Although King David penned the words centuries ago, they fell fresh on my heart that day at the dining room table. The words "brokenhearted" and "crushed in spirit" perfectly described my mood. But there was good news, too. The Lord was close, and He would save me.

Up until this point, my relationship with God was based on head knowledge alone. I had graduated from a Christian college. I believed. I had always believed, but now I knew more was necessary. God was calling me deeper.

I had come to the end of myself, and doctors provided no hope. My fear of going deeper with the Lord dissolved as I felt the words of Scripture tear down walls built over a lifetime.

The Holy Spirit moved in. The Bible came alive as never before. I realized God wasn't mad at me, or punishing me. The entire planet is under a curse . . . our bodies included. Death is inevitable, but God is in the midst of the broken. He felt my pain and entered into it.

A crazy thought took root in my brain: *Maybe I can do this blindness thing with God's help.* For the first time, a ray of hope poked through the gloom. A future seemed possible.

I prayed in earnest, and God brought committed Christian women into my life. I heard three simple words — "Jesus loves you" — and they no longer felt like a cliché. I found a Bible-believing church and got baptized. The pastor's wife asked me to speak at a women's gathering. There, an older saint specifically prayed for writing opportunities to open up for me. A short time later, a shy friend said she felt led by God to tell me about a ministry seeking proofreaders for devotions. I applied and got the position.

These days I sit in front of a large screen television monitor, which doubles as a computer screen. I have published many articles. I have proofread many devotions and continue on my writing journey — albeit slowly.

Over the past fuzzy years of walking with God, I have learned that His love is far different than a Hollywood script. It is so much deeper and more surprising than the turn of a man-made plot.

Like the messy bird's nest I recently discovered outside the window near my desk, God's love is uniquely formed for my situation. It's personal.

Sometimes I marvel that twenty years have passed since my diagnosis. I remember how long and difficult the days were at first. I remember saying, "I can't live like this."

Now I know, with the Lord's presence, "I can live like this."

Although my physical sight is now worse than before, my spiritual vision is 20/20. When I look down on the bird's nest, I don't see a mess. Instead, I see four fragile blue eggs huddled close. I watch the mother bird coming and going, carefully tending her clutch. I see new life about to burst forth, and I smile at the irony of God placing this nest where only I can see it.

13

Lee Has Cancer

Rob Buck

Lee and I grew up together on the same street. On summer days we'd hop on our bikes and pedal down to Shaw's pharmacy and spend our allowance on baseball cards and fire balls. We played countless basketball games at each other's court, swam at the community pool and played on the same little league team.

We endured our parents' divorces during our formative years, leaving us both on shaky ground. Neither of our fathers had the capacity to help us navigate manhood, so we did the best we could. We tried to live good lives, but eventually followed our friends into experimenting with smoking and drinking. Once this began, the tide took us deeper into drugs and other misdeeds. Lee quit high school and joined the army. I went to college.

While in college, I pursued worldly pleasures I thought would bring me joy. As a result, I almost lost a scholarship my mother had worked hard to secure. During fifty-cent beer night, I was arrested for DUI. As I sat in jail before my buddies bailed me out, I realized my life was on a downward trajectory. I knew I needed God, I but didn't know how to approach Him. My experience with "born again" Christians seemed to be a life of joyless rules.

In the meantime, Lee was on a similar downward spiral. He landed in jail for drug possession in California. During the incident, he was introduced to Jesus Christ as a personal Savior, not a rule-demanding killjoy. His life was truly changed and he couldn't wait to tell me.

One day, when Lee was on furlough and I was home for the weekend, he asked me, "Robby, do you think you're going to heaven?"

"Yeah," I replied.

"How do you know?"

"I believe in Jesus, like it says in the Bible," I replied. "I haven't killed anybody and I've lived a pretty good life."

"But the Bible says you'll know them by their fruit."

This took me back. I certainly wasn't living a life of good fruit.

"If you want joy." Lee continued. "Your priorities need to be Jesus first, then others and finally yourself."

"Lee, I'd need to clean my life up first before I could give my life to Jesus."

"Do you take a bath before you take a shower?" he asked. "Jesus will accept a person exactly where they are."

My conversation with Lee was one of the primary seeds God used to bring me to my knees months later. In late summer of 1977, I admitted to the Lord I'd made a mess of my life. I accepted what He'd done on the cross on my behalf and received His life in exchange for my sin. I had no idea what to do next, but my life in Christ had begun.

Lee and I have remained close for almost sixty years now. We realize how rare our friendship is and we don't take it for granted. It's extremely comforting to have a bud who's been in your life for as long as you can remember, especially when life gets hard.

I got a call from Lee last month informing me there is a lump on his chest. They'd be doing a biopsy soon to see if it's cancerous. He seemed to be handling it well, but my heart sank. *Not Lee. Lord, please not cancer.*

The following week he found out he has breast cancer. He told me the plan is to be determined, but he didn't want to waste this opportunity to magnify the Lord in this very difficult situation.

Lee is one of my heroes. Not only did he care enough to share God's good news with me, but he models what it looks like to care more about God's glory than his own welfare.

Yes, and I will rejoice, for I know that this will turn out for my deliverance through your prayers and the provision of the Spirit of Jesus Christ, according to my earnest expectation and hope, that I will not be put to shame in anything, but that with all boldness, Christ will even now, as always, be exalted in my body, whether by life or by death. For to me, to live is Christ and to die is gain" (Philippians 1:18b-21 NASB).

He walks in the fact that his wellbeing is tied to his closeness to God, not his circumstances.

* * *

Lord, I thank you for my friend Lee. I cherish his friendship over all these many years. In Christ, I have bold access to your throne. I know You're able to heal Lee. Will You, please. Also, please honor his request to allow his cancer to glorify You. Use it to bring people closer to You. Draw near to Lee in the early morning hours when he needs to know You're there. I pray these things in the faithful name of Jesus the Christ.

14

He Knows My Name

Jeri McBryde

My hands trembled as I opened the envelope. The letter started out so polite and friendly. "Thank you for your recent visit to our facility." The second sentence started a roller coaster of emotions. "Your exam shows the need for further evaluation." The rest was a blur.

Later that day, I followed the letter's instructions and made an appointment with the Hospital Mammography Center.

On the day of the appointment, I made my way to the admission desk. This time I was directed past the routine screening side and sent to the diagnostic team. I was too old for this.

The waiting area was quiet. There was not much talking, just a group of silent, scared women wrapped in fluffy white bathrobes, their thoughts on the future. Soft music and the soothing and relaxing sound of water flowing down a rock wall fountain brought a feeling of calmness. I glanced around at the paintings and sculptures that decorated the room. Each had a small, engraved plaque in memory of someone.

Well, that's encouraging, I thought.

They called my name. I followed the nurse down a long, cold hallway, passing doctors, patients, nurses, and technicians. I entered a scary world of digital diagnostic mammograms, ultrasounds, bone scans, biopsies, and heaven knows what else.

Then the words no one wants to hear, "You have cancer." My heart sank. *Not again.* A mixture of emotions flooded over me. I was overwhelmed, shocked, afraid, and very mad. So many questions, the decision of where to go to begin my journey of treatment and healing. A journey I had traveled before.

I was blessed to live near a large city known for its medical care and award-winning hospitals. There were several exceptional cancer centers with excellent reputations.

Everyone had an opinion of where I should go.

"Please, dear God," I silently cried. "Tell me what to do, where to go." Tears ran down my face as I reached out in prayer. "Please, Lord, put me on a healing path. Show me the way."

Suddenly I noticed this beautiful inscription on the wall above the checkout counter. It read: "I know the plans I have for you, declares the Lord. Plans for Hope and a Future. Jer. 29:11."

My eyeglasses weren't on and I had tears in my eyes. However, I kept reading the words. "Look," I called to my husband. "This has my name on it. It says 'Jeri.'"

He came over and studied the writing. "It's J-e-r," he said. "That's the abbreviation for Jeremiah. The words are the biblical verse in Jeremiah 29:11. That's not an '*i*' after Jer. It's a period."

That was his interpretation. To me, it still said *Jeri*. "I know the plans I have for you, declares the Lord. Plans for Hope and a Future, Jeri."

I looked up at the wall. There was no doubt in my mind. I was going to stay here. I knew God was in control and that everything would be okay. I wasn't afraid of dying, I knew my final destination. I just wasn't ready to say goodbye. There were so many things I wanted to experience. I wanted to see my children settled and happy, the marriage of my only granddaughter, so many things.

I was thrilled to be given a notebook with tabs. There were sections for Breast Care and Office Information, Doctors, Treatment Plans, Hormonal Therapy, Radiation, Surgery, Tests, Medicine, and finally, Follow-Up Care.

I instantly went into research mode. I started with the doctor who would do my surgery and manage my care. Her education and credentials were excellent. But what stood out was her answer to the survey question: What can a patient expect when they have you as a doctor?

Her response: My patients can expect compassionate care.

Last but not least was my oncologist. He, too, had excellent credentials. His survey question: What could I expect with him as a doctor?

His response: "Empathy and sensitivity to the patient's situation, personalization of each patient's care, being forthright, respectful, and thorough." I knew he would become my new best friend when I read his patient reviews. "He sits and really listens to you and makes you feel safe and that everything will be okay."

I was at peace after researching and choosing my doctors. I was no longer worried. I felt hopeful. I was in the right place.

After all, the Lord has plans for me. He told me so. He wrote it on the wall, "Plans for Hope and a Future, Jeri." He knows my name.

15

Eighteen Days

By Bob Blundell

"How long?" I asked.

They hesitated. "Everyone is different," one said. "But most *expire* within two weeks."

The word hovered in the air like a callous reference to forgotten milk.

I prayed for a quicker end. But that would not be the case. The two weeks had come and gone. Then another day followed, and another after that. In all, seventeen days had passed and as the eighteenth arrived, I wondered if I would be able to summon the strength to go on.

Sunlight filtered through smudged windows and I gazed out at the city wondering, "Why didn't God just end this? What purpose could be served by prolonging his suffering?"

But there would be no clap of thunder or flash of light from the heavens. The machines, the wires, instruments to prolong a life no human would ever want — they were all gone now. That decision made eighteen days before.

This morning family and friends had come to say their goodbyes. Most hurried quickly past his bedside, perhaps preferring to remember him as he once was rather than what lay before them. Finally, as the last of them filed through the doorway, the room became silent again.

Now, it was just me, a chair on each side of a bed in a spartan room, and my dying father. He and I would see things through to the end. Together.

His frail body was a shadow of what he had once been. Like a thin layer of parchment, translucent skin stretched over muscle and bone, the profile of each awkward corner and turn of the human body, now visible. Earlier, his breath had come in gasps like a drowning swimmer desperate to survive. But now, with the drugs to keep him comfortable and the end approaching, he was calm.

The Book in my lap was opened to Psalms 23. The words I had repeated hour after hour should have given me strength. But my only feeling was of despair and a dark sense of helplessness.

Occasionally a young face would peek through the door. "Do you need anything? Please let us know if anything changes."

But today, *change* meant something entirely different.

I lay the Bible on the bedside table and watched the slow, rhythmic rise and fall of his chest, the movement barely discernible to the human eye. My eyes closed and a kaleidoscope of memories flashed through my mind.

Ours had been a tumultuous relationship, six decades fraught with emotional hills and valleys. We were both strong-willed and for much of that time we had pushed each other away in anger or hurt. But as time passed, the walls we had so carefully constructed began to erode, and what I remember now are the last ten years we had together. Those days will always be cherished, as we had put aside our differences and learned to love each other again as father and son.

When I opened my eyes, something compelled me to stand and go to his bedside. I settled in beside him, studying his face, then took his withered hand in mine and squeezed. I draped an arm around his thin shoulders, once broad and muscled, and put my lips to his ear.

"Dad," I whispered. "It's okay to stop fighting now. It's okay to let go."

Then I sensed a change. I touched his wrist lightly and a bittersweet wave of emotion washed over me. I knew God had him now.

* * *

Twenty miles outside the city of Austin is a lightly-traveled road known as the Devil's Backbone. It winds through rolling hills sprinkled with cedar, mesquite trees, and cactus. During better times we would go there to enjoy the visual splendor of God's artistry.

Dusk was approaching, and I sat alone in a secluded park overlooking the hillside. The sun had begun its slow melt into the horizon, casting an amber glow over the valley. It shone like a freshly-minted penny.

As shadows fell around me, a cool northerly wind caressed my face, and I was suddenly struck by the significance of what had happened. To the extent any human mind can comprehend God's ways, I could now see His plan for my father and me.

I had been given an incredible gift. The Lord allowed me to hold my father in my arms as he drew his last breath in this world. Those years of anger and separation between us melted away, and I buried my face in my palms and wept until there were no more tears to cry.

16

Laughter from God

Janet Ann Collins

I tend to worry a lot.

When I learned I had Ocular Melanoma — a rare kind of cancer — in my eye and the treatment might make me lose the vision in it, I asked the people in my church to pray that I wouldn't worry.

Still, the next day I was worrying while outside walking my dog. But a tune kept running through my head. At first I couldn't recognize it, but then I realized it was the melody from the song "The Purple People Eater" — "it was a one-eyed, one-horned, flyin' purple people eater."

From then on, every time I started to worry I'd think of that song and laugh instead.

Because my tumor was way down in the corner of my eye I didn't loose any vision from the proton beam radiation treatment, but even if I had become "one-eyed" I would have trusted God and laughed instead of worrying.

God must have a sense of humor.

17

Intercession

Steve Carter

The sudden gust from the eighteen-wheeler and the noise of the massive engine blowing by shook me to the core, but my fright was short-lived. A quick, friendly blast from the truck's air horn signaled approval of the large American flag flying from my trike.

This late night encouragement, along with cheering, friendly waves, and a television interview, all since I had started in International Falls, Minnesota, supported my reason for peddling from "Canada to Key West, Florida."

I initially planned the trip for the sake of scenery and to "test my mettle" physically and mentally. However, in light of the lack of respect being shown nationwide for our flag, I decided to fly a larger one as a statement of thanks to our military veterans and to display my fierce patriotism.

Now, after twelve hours of peddling on my recumbent trike, I found myself drifting into traffic because I could no longer focus. In the wake of the near miss, I immediately pulled over. This close encounter made it obvious I had put myself in extreme danger. After setting the hand brakes, I stumbled upright, stepped over the wheels, and reviewed the events leading to my predicament.

Riding through southern Missouri had proven much more physically and mentally taxing than I had anticipated. This section of my "Canada to Key West Ride" blessed me abundantly while simultaneously exposing me to a depth of misery I had never before experienced. Many long days peddling, followed by inadequate rest in seedy motels, had caught up with me. Poor nutrition, consisting of mostly peanut butter, crackers, and sports drinks, was taking a toll on my endurance, thus slowing my attempt at dodging the day's heat.

Immediately after a pre-dawn start, my legs still tired, problems had set in with the endless, steep hills. Although my knees were supported by braces, my hands had soon begun to cramp from constant gear changing and braking. After nearly stalling when I ran out of gears, I'd anticipated a flat tire. Finally, I had set the brakes, climbed off the trike, stumbled around, and poked the tires. I had been happy that I didn't have to fix a flat, but my spirits had sagged a little because my legs were already all but exhausted.

Morning had passed quickly before I reached the southbound four-lane road that pointed me toward Memphis. Although I was markedly happier with my own lane to ride in, the improvement came at a price. Instead of small-town traffic and confusing road signs, very large, fast-moving trucks now kept me company. Motels and places to buy nutrition had become increasingly scarce . . . which could lead to low blood sugar and dehydration.

Normally, when riding over terrain like what graced this part of Missouri, I restricted my mileage to under eighty miles a day. Unfortunately, the state's rural countryside lacked ample lodging and convenience stores. Now, with darkness fast approaching, my supplies a fading memory, aching legs all but dead, and over thirty miles between me and the next motel, I felt an unfamiliar dread.

I unclipped my shoes from the pedals and struggled to stand. In an effort to regain circulation to my lower extremities, I stumbled around, wondering if falling into the road or a ditch would win out.

Although I normally relied on my own strength during times of duress, tonight I realized from experience gleaned while peddling twice across the country that I was in serious trouble.

My recumbent trike consists of a seat the size of a lawn chair, three wheels to keep me from falling over, and handle bars for steering. Having napped on it numerous times, I knew it would be more comfortable than sleeping in a ditch. Scanning the surrounding underbrush and trees, I began to plan a night sleeping on my trike.

That's when I suddenly felt God thump me on the head.

"Call the church."

I pulled my phone out and hit speed dial.

Brother Reggie, who was on call that night, answered. As soon as I heard his voice, I knew everything was going to be all right because that man is a prayer warrior of the highest order. I told him about my dire straits, which grabbed his attention. Reggie did not just say "I'll pray for you," and go back to watching television like many would have. This man of God went to work immediately praying an intercessory prayer on my behalf. Afterwards, I knew God had answered our plea.

Strength and spirit renewed, I thanked him repeatedly.

He responded, "When I heard the ring, I almost didn't answer, but God told me to."

I assured him we would talk again soon and I headed south, leaning into the remaining three hours of hills.

After a mile or two, I spotted the lights of a convenience store glowing in the darkness about a half mile off the highway. I'm convinced God's timing had a hand in my seeing that place; I probably would have missed it in the daylight due to concealing trees.

While stocking up I, must have been a pitiful sight because several people offered me food and shelter. But with rain in the next day's forecast, I acknowledged their courtesy and got back on the road.

My legs' strength was renewed following Reggie's prayer, and I steadily ground out the remaining miles into Poplar Bluff, Missouri. The miles however were not, by any stretch of the imagination, easy. Large trucks roared past me on the fog-shrouded highway. Confusing road signs and an almost-dead phone battery made navigation even more difficult. But just before midnight, after one-hundred thirteen miles, I rolled into the lobby of the motel I had booked.

Following a much-needed shower, I gave thought to how the day had given me a better understanding of intercessory prayer. For nearly twenty-five years had I suffered with Meniere's syndrome, an inner-ear disease. Despite numerous prayers for healing, I'd endured multiple surgeries, trips to emergency rooms, and vertigo-induced bicycle crashes, all of which God could have prevented but didn't. These struggles challenged my faith as I participated in several ministries and strived to be a good father and husband.

Enduring sickness for so much of my life had left me skeptical about the effectiveness of intercessory prayer. However, after experiencing the miracle of renewed leg strength and the unexpected nutrition I was able to purchase, I gained great insight into the wisdom of following the guidance of the Holy Spirit.

Thankfully, I had obeyed God's prompting and called Reggie for help. Answering the phone displayed Reggie's servant's heart, which prompted a mighty, heartfelt prayer. As a result, God heard our prayer and answered, giving me renewed physical and mental strength, as well as nourishment for my body.

I'll never know for certain what would have been the cost of ignoring God's instructions to call the church that miserable evening in Missouri. My fate without Reggie being guided to answer the phone is anybody's guess. However, I'm convinced without our obedience and Reggie's powerful prayer, my time on earth could well have ended on that dark hostile road in the Missouri hills.

18

The Voice Within

Lola Di Giulio De Maci

Christmas was less than a week away, and I was ready. Tree trimmed. Gifts wrapped. Cookies baked. But in between all my busyness, a familiar voice within my heart said, "Listen to me."

I soon recognized the voice as the same voice I had heard somewhere deep inside me seventeen years earlier. I called my doctor immediately and made an appointment. I appeared in his office within a week.

He asked, "Did you receive the letter I sent my patients saying I was retiring?"

"No. I had no idea that this would be your last day." I had been putting off making an appointment for my annual physical. I was grateful that I called before he was gone.

Twenty-four years ago I was diagnosed with breast cancer. I had left the doctor's office with a clean bill of health only to return three weeks later. I was hurrying onto the playground on my way to the teacher's room one morning when I hit my breast on the steel handle of the entry gate. The next morning I noticed a bruise and called my doctor. I thought I'd better check it out.

"Did you hit yourself in the exact spot of the bruise?" he asked.

"Yes, in the exact spot."

"I feel a thickness in the breast," he said.

"A thickness?" I repeated, echoing his words. "It wasn't there three weeks ago."

"I'd like to do a biopsy just to be certain it's nothing more than a bruise."

A biopsy? I felt chills run up and down my spine.

"To err on the side of caution," he assured me.

The following day I'd had the biopsy. The surgeon found a lump in the scar tissue that had formed from the bruise. As I opened the gate, I had hit myself in the exact spot where a malignant tumor had been growing for about two years. The thickness the doctor had felt in my breast was scar tissue. Through all this, I wasn't aware that I was walking through a miracle until I was on the other side of it. I called it "Divine Intervention."

My surgeon has asked me repeatedly over the years, "What made you come in?"

"A voice within," I would reply. Something inside me told me that something wasn't right.

And now here I was again following that voice inside me.

"I'm sorry, Lola," he said, this time. "We've found a cancer in your uterus."

I listened to the doctor, my heart racing.

"I'm shocked," he continued. "The cancer was completely unexpected, as well as barely detectable. There must have been a third power in the exam room with us that day. This is a miracle."

A third power? A miracle? These words seared my very core. I searched my soul. "Perhaps it was God. Or my infant daughter who left me for heaven. I'm not sure."

I faced a second cancer surgeon for the second time in seventeen years.

"I don't know if it was God or your baby, but it definitely was someone," she said. "You told me that you had no symptoms?"

"None. Just a voice within me telling me that something wasn't right."

"Do you have courage?" she asked.

"No," I said right out. I sat there motionless. I didn't blink. I didn't move. *Here we go again,* my mind kept repeating. I didn't know if I could go through this again.

"Yes!" I suddenly blurted out. "I do have courage." I figured, since

I'd lived through all I had to do to save my life the first time, I could do it again.

The surgery was set for six a.m. on Ash Wednesday. I thought it rather a coincidence that my first cancer surgery had been performed at six p.m. on Good Friday. Then I remembered, there is no coincidence with God. He orchestrates everything.

My cancer had been discovered early enough that I did not need treatment." *What are the chances of that?* I asked myself many times over.

I have often wondered if the same power that propelled me into a gate one school day morning was the same one that invited itself into an exam room shortly before Christmas seven years ago.

What I do know for sure is that I have lived beyond twenty-four years as a two-time cancer survivor. I take each day and live it as best I can, making each morning a brand-new beginning — a personal promise of new life.

New Beginnings. New Life. Twenty-four years and counting.

God had truly opened a gate and my heart to a miracle.

19

My Faith Still Holds

Diana Leagh Matthews

Listening to the raspy voice of my once strong father, my mind drifts back almost two decades ago. The song is referring to finding life's mysteries and having a childlike faith.

"Daddy preached this morning. He announced his cancer is in remission. Then said whether it returned tomorrow, next week, next month, next year, in five years or never he would trust God. He ended by singing *My Faith Still Holds*." Mama shared when she called that long-ago Sunday afternoon.

"Is he still going to Jacksonville next week?" He would see an oncology specialist the following week.

"Yes. I hurt my back. Can you drive us?"

"I believe I can squeeze it in." Two days earlier I had been laid off three weeks early as I prepared to move an hour away to start college as an adult student. Maybe this was the reason.

The next day I drove the three hours to my parents' house. Daddy served the church they were at only a year before his diagnosis, but what a blessing this church was. We would leave the next morning for the eight-hour drive to Jacksonville, Florida.

Daddy may have announced the doctor's diagnosis of remission, but I wasn't sure. The slightest sound bothered him, and he tired easily. If he was in remission, why wasn't he feeling better?

Daddy's inability to stand a lot of noise or conversation made for a very long ride. In order to keep myself awake and occupied while driving, I mentally reviewed the family history I'd been working on.

"Get over." Daddy sat in the passenger's seat and directed me the entire way. "Now get back over in that lane."

I bit my tongue. He was only trying to help. Now was not the time to smart off. This must be even more difficult on him than to the rest of us.

By the time we arrived in Jacksonville, Daddy was exhausted. He rested in the hotel while Mama and I went in search of something to eat. By the time we returned he was asleep.

The doctors gave us no real answers on that visit, but I'll never forget those extra days with my parents.

On the ride home, we stopped at Cracker Barrel, where Daddy ordered meatloaf and mashed potatoes. We had no idea this would be the last real meal he would enjoy.

I visited another day or two, before returning home to finish packing. Besides, I would be back in less than a fortnight for my birthday.

On the drive home, I thought over all the changes we'd endured in the past year. A year ago, Daddy was healthy, other than some swelling in his legs. The doctors never provided answers for this swelling and we believe it was related to his eventual diagnosis, even if the doctors didn't agree. Daddy developed a growth under his arm which the doctor operated on and biopsied a few weeks before Thanksgiving. The news came back with the dreaded word. Cancer.

I was at work when Mama called me with the news. I couldn't comprehend it. My healthy father couldn't have cancer, but he did. Over Thanksgiving break he tried to prepare me for the possibility of losing him, but I wasn't ready. After all he would be fifty in a few short months, my two younger siblings were still at home and he was serving the Lord through ministry. Why would the Lord take him now?

As much as I didn't want to think about the inevitable, the thought continued to play in my mind. Would this be our last holiday season together? I strived to cherish each moment we were together. Daddy was tired and weak from the daily chemotherapy and radiation treatments, but he pushed himself to spend time with the family over Christmas. As a new millennium was ushered in, we watched the celebrations taking place around the world. When the clock tolled midnight in a different country, Mama walked over to Daddy, resting in his recliner, and they kissed in the new year. Each hour they carried out this routine.

While I drove home I prayed for Daddy to be healed, and a happier time. Daddy promised next Easter we would perform the cantata he compiled and I looked forward to worshipping the Lord and performing together.

Mama called the following day with the news Daddy was back in the hospital.

Will he be home when I return for my birthday?

The doctors weren't sure, and I couldn't imagine not having Daddy there. I talked with Mama daily, but the news was not encouraging.

Two weeks later, I returned home in time to assist Daddy into the house.

Lacey, our black cocker spaniel, stood at the door wagging her tail on his return home. We settled him into his recliner, and she went over and laid down beside him.

My heart broke watching pain cross his face. I would give anything to see him well and active again. Even simple activities, such as getting up, wore him out and he stayed in bed or in his recliner. I limited my visits to a few moments at a time. I missed the days we would sit and talk or he would tell me about his childhood and grandparents.

For my birthday supper, Daddy made the effort to join the rest of the family at the table. Sitting there took every ounce of strength he possessed, but he wanted to make the day special for me. I don't remember anything else about that meal other than he was there.

I kissed Daddy goodbye, two days later. I was returning home with a move ahead of me later that week, while he headed back to the doctor.

"He's been admitted back to the hospital." Mama said when I called to let her know I arrived home safely.

Tears ran down my cheek. Daddy was home for four days before heading back to the hospital. The four days I was home to celebrate my birthday.

After moving, I made the hour-long journey to the hospital the day before classes began. As I kissed Daddy goodbye I had no idea this was the last time I would see him on this side of heaven.

I struggled to get into my new routine with school and a new job, but my mind lingered on Daddy. I continued to call and leave messages for Mama, not understanding why we could not connect.

A week after seeing Daddy, I discovered the voice mail system on my new landline and the messages from Mama detailing the gradual decline.

"The doctors are starting an experimental drug."

"Daddy is in a coma."

"The kids came today. It was all they could do to see Daddy."

I crawled into a ball as I listened to the messages.

"The doctor's said he will either fly or die today. You may want to come see him."

I gathered an overnight bag, while leaving messages for Mama. Picking up my purse and bag, my hand on the door a strange tone sounded. I went in search of the unfamiliar noise to discover it was my new phone. Soon I discovered why I'd not been able to get calls for a week.

"Daddy died fifteen minutes ago." Mama's voice broke. "Earlier today he opened his eyes and looked straight up. I know he was looking at Jesus or the angels. Then he closed his eyes and slipped back into the coma."

I sank onto the floor, clutching the phone in disbelief. My strong father couldn't be gone. I looked around my still empty living room in disbelief, reaching for the nearest item, a phone book, before throwing it across the bare floor. "Why?" I screamed over and over. I was in a bad dream.

"Why couldn't it be me?" Papa asked several days later.

I wondered the same. Not that I didn't love my Papa, but he was experiencing the early signs of dementia. Daddy was only fifty and still serving the Lord. I didn't understand.

As we stood in the receiving line, we had a small glimpse of his impact as numerous comments were made on his faith.

"I can't tell you what a blessing he was to me."

"He really ministered to my heart while we received chemo together."

"His faith was a testimony in itself."

"He led me to the Lord while I had chemotherapy."

Although Daddy didn't understand why he was sick at this time, he had faith in the Lord and His plan.

As I played our signature song, *We Shall Behold Him*, for his memorial service my mind thought about how he was beholding the Lord at that moment. I realized the unexpected ways the Lord blessed me, by providing the opportunity to drive him to Jacksonville and have him home for my birthday.

My faith still holds onto the Christ of Calvary.

I'm brought back the present. Daddy's voice quivers, as he finishes the song which talks of putting trust in things that cannot be seen.

Even after all this time, Daddy and I continue to connect over our shared love of music. I still don't understand why, but I know Daddy's journey was a testimony to so many others.

He struggled with leaving behind his family but was not afraid to meet the Lord he loved and served so faithfully.

As the song ends, I'm reminded none of us had an idea this sermon and song would be Daddy's last. He'd only preached when he was able those last nine months of his illness, but he was living out a greater sermon for others, who might never hear him preach, to witness.

I would give anything to have Daddy with us again and to perform together one more time. Mama and I often discuss what he might be like now or his opinion on current events. Then there are the numerous questions I want to ask him, including how much did you struggle before surrendering to place your faith in the Lord's plan.

I may never understand why but one day I will see Daddy again and we will be able to sing together for an eternity. On that day, I will have all the answers and can ask him all the questions I want. Not because he will join me, but because I will join him and the Lord.

Daddy left an enduring legacy. One of faith and love. Even in the years when I rebelled after his death, his testimony lingered in the back of my mind and spoke to my heart, before I surrendered my own faith.

One day as I walk into his outstretched arms I'll say, "Thank you, Daddy, for having a faith that holds and resting on the Christ of Calvary. You taught me how to walk in faith."

Does your faith still hold to the blessed Rock of Ages and the Christ of Calvary?

20

The Green Envelope

Tanja Dufrene

It was a good exercise, engaging both the mind and motor skills. Yet what was the purpose? Why did the Spirit prompt me to copy specific scriptures to index cards? Hesitantly, I acted on His prompting. When the coming weeks turned our lives upside down, revelation soon followed. It was cancer. There were too many tests to deny it.

A whirlwind of doctor's visits, consults, meetings, and planning sessions blew through our lives with the violent fury of a tornado. The information was overwhelming, the possibilities staggering. Thankfully, answers arose as one day led into the next. Yet we were running on sheer adrenaline and shock.

Within a very short time we were checking into the hospital where life-altering surgery would be performed. Yet God had proved faithful through each step, each decision, each dilemma. Now we were acting on the best advice we had received while trusting God to guide us through.

I heard they advised my family the surgery went well, quicker than expected. Yes, God was there, guiding the hands of the surgeons, whispering to the medical staff, and leading each in how to complete their tasks for success. But my first memory was lying on a bed being rolled through a hallway and feeling the greatest pain I had ever known. Immediately words burst through my lips in an attempt to garner attention and help: "Pain! Pain! Pain! Pain!" I had had surgery in the past and knew I should be feeling groggy, lethargic, even restful, but most certainly not like I wanted to give up just to escape the Pain! For some reason, the anesthesia wore off before the pain medication took effect.

The hours that followed were filled with every attempt I could make to divert my focus from the pain. All the medical interventions administered just could not seem to get ahead of the pain. I cried. I prayed. I begged. I worshipped. I wriggled around in the bed.

Not wanting anyone to see me in such pain, I asked that my husband not be allowed in the room with me. But he insisted. He sat there in the corner, concerned no doubt. He knew he belonged there. And what a blessing he was to me.

In time and in His ever-gentle ways, the Holy Spirit reminded me of the green envelope. I had given it to our daughter just before we left for the hospital, asking her to hold it in her purse for safekeeping. I finally asked my husband to retrieve the envelope and read the scriptures to me that I had been led to write on the index cards. God's Word has always been a special comfort, even when nothing else could calm me. He read, and read. Still the pain pursued, threating my physical and mental well-being.

Eventually, his voice began to give way. His words were harder to hear. So he asked if I would allow our daughter to come in and read to me. Desperate for anything that might bring relief, I agreed. She came in the room and read to me. Her voice was strong, yet disquieted. She could sense the intensity with which I was desperately holding on to hope. She read. I prayed. I hurt. I cried. My greatest efforts were failing. Nothing seemed to bring relief. I began to doubt my ability to continue. All I could think of was relief from the pain. Then He spoke: "When people are in pain, they look for the quickest way out."

In that moment, I knew it was true. I was looking for anything to bring relief. But nothing was working.

Then the sounds changed. She began to sing songs of worship. Each melody was calming to my mind and spirit, even if my body refused to respond. Then she came to the side of the bed and began caressing my face with her delicate hand. Finally, there was something upon which my mind could focus. Her voice was angelic. His touch through her was calming even though the pain continued through the night.

After several hours, she exited, and my husband played worship music on my phone. With the passing of time, the music would stop. Hesitantly, I would wake him to reset it. Sleep eluded me. Pain pursued me. Yet peace fill the room as praise filled the space.

In time we were released to return home, even though the pain continued. It would be weeks before my body calmed and my mind eased. But God walked through each step with me and my family. The pain was real. It was ominous and threatening. But it did not overpower. Even when I thought I would not survive, God was watching and did not let me go where I did not belong. He still has a plan and purpose for me. And I want to fulfill it. He knew the green envelope would be needed. He placed a key in there for us to retrieve at just the right moment.

So what about you? What seemingly simple or silly tasks might the Spirit be prompting you to do? With what will you fill your green envelope, that symbolic "Go To" when the pain of life seems greater than your strength?

> *But as for me, I watch in hope for the Lord,*
> *I wait for God my Savior; my God will hear me.*
>
> Micah 7:7 NIV

21

The Last Chapter

Brenda Miller

We spend our years as a tale that is told.

Psalm 90:9b KJV

Other versions of the Scriptures speak of the end of our years with the descriptive words *sigh*, *moan*, or *groan*. I experienced this when the last breath of life slipped from the lungs of my mother and my husband. My heart that was crushed, and I groaned from deep within me.

However, as I read the King James Version, I envision an open biography. Before we inhale one breath, God has written our biographies, ordained our purposes. (See Psalm 56:8.)

In my vision, this biography contains chapters. As I review my own life, I can divide it into chapters, or seasons as some might say. My future is still a "tale to be told" — years or days to be lived. My ministry and mission have yet to be completed.

Yes, our days are numbered, and our times are in God's hands (Psalm 31:15), but that does not mean that God does not have the power to use His eraser or make a new entry.

This story is not about me. When I began the dreaded task of selecting a monument for my husband's grave, I began to think about the "last chapter" of his life. The etchings, names, and dates on stones told stories and reminded me of the chapters we had spent together in almost fifty years of marriage. The first few chapters were filled with love, dreams, hope, and our children's births.

However, we don't live in the Garden of Eden. Mankind was banished because of disobedience to God's laws. So life happens, and we make choices. Some consequences create less-enjoyable chapters: The flames of love flicker. Pleasant dreams turn into nightmares. Hope fades into fear, failure, and rejection. Our children aren't so cute and cuddly any more. But then there are the grandchildren and great-grandchildren!

The last chapter of Tommy's life began on April 17, 2018. He came home mid-afternoon from work, exhausted, and experiencing an excruciating pain in his left ribcage. He lived with pain in his back and neck. Occasional UTI complications due to bladder resection caused additional pain. But he had never experienced severe pain in this location.

After enduring back surgery, three episodes of cancer, and a major heart attack, I didn't waste any time getting him to the doctor's office and on to the hospital.

For the next twelve weeks we lived his last chapter in and out of the hospital, desperately hoping we could win this last battle with cancer. We began with the attitude of "we can" but one crisis after another threatened our positive attitude. Crucial decisions bombarded us — then me. Truly, we had nowhere to go but to the "Lord God of truth" (Psalm 31:5 kjv).

The enemies of my husband's body attacked him with unbearable pain, which required the most powerful medications available. We didn't so much mind the "high" state of mind, because he was the funny daddy. But the health care professionals couldn't risk an overdose, so they also used other medications that kept him sedated. Our daughters worked during the day, so I was mostly alone with my sleeping husband until they came in the afternoon.

During that time, my only view of the world was through windows, the shades opened to allow in light and a view of the activities of people on the streets. Inside I heard the sounds of shoes thudding in the halls, nurses communicating, and other patients complaining or talking to visitors.

Feelings of uncertainty, uneasiness, and unanswered questions were always present. I couldn't fast forward the pages of Tommy's story. What did the future hold?

I thought: *Each day will have its own description — hopeful, stormy, sunny, lonely. Who decides the description? God numbers our days, but how many are left?* (See Psalm 90:10.) I received no answer. *Quantity is out of our control,* I thought. *But, what about the quality of those days? Can we still make a difference?*

One setback after another seemed to block the view.

What about our choices? One doctor urged Tommy to make a decision about resuscitation procedures. The oncologist pressed for decisions on more treatment options. My husband wasn't ready to make those decisions, but we did try every option that became available. Yet nothing seemed to give hope or relieve his never-ending pain.

One day, as I opened the shades and peered through the windows, the sun was rising over the tall buildings, and the clouds circled and floated away. *God is still in control of His creation, and I am grateful for another day to live in faith. God is merciful. He placed Tommy in such a restful state that he never stirred during the hour-long search for an IV site.*

I thought of Jesus sleeping in the boat while His disciples were fearfully anxious, and shaking Jesus until He awoke. They wanted His power to deliver them, but, like me, they really needed to experience the mercy and grace of the Father God.

God is our refuge and strength, a helper who is always found in times of trouble (Psalm 46:1 CSB).

The life support question was broached again, and again Tommy avoided the subject. He didn't want to speak of death. His mind could only accept so much reality, especially when it was negative — terminal.

The hospital housed cubicle after cubicle of people: the patients, caregivers, specialists, lifesavers, management, maintenance, food service — an arena of sadness, sorrow, pain, healing, and the occasional "Hallelujah!"

Special people walked through those doors every day, I discovered, ready to confront the many facets of living and dying.

Another day, a different view of the skyline revealed heavy, dense fog. The beauty of God's creation was draped in gloominess, gray and red concrete. Only a few reminders of God's breath rose from the small amount of earth that was visible. The weather condition mirrored my mindset. I needed to see evidence of God's spoken Word, His life-giving breath of knowledge, power, and His presence.

I wondered how we could make decisions when we'd only read the pages of our biographies to the present and didn't know what's on the additional pages. Everybody was trying to write Tommy's life story. I prayed Psalm 119:147: *I rise before dawn and cry out for help; I have put my hope in your word* (NIV).

When Tommy was no longer able to make decisions for his future, palliative measures seemed the only solution. The oncologist still pushed for treatment but my husband's body would not cooperate.

"I don't know how to flip the pages," Tommy cried. The children and I had to guide him to make end-of-life plans for living with dignity and comfort.

I prayed for the Spirit to break through, dispel the fog in our minds, clarify our understanding and deliver Tommy from destructive thoughts. The message of Psalm 119:169, *"Let my cry reach you, Lord; give me understanding according to your word"* (CSB) became personal. We pleaded for the last pages of Tommy's story to be full of love, joy, and peace, the true gifts of the Spirit!

I prayed for God's mercy to deliver my husband from the agony of fighting for a few more days. W pleaded that he would be comfortable and focused on eternal life, not the last grueling effects of death on earth.

Eternal life was his destination, but I hoped we were testifying to our faith in God and the saving grace of our Lord Jesus Christ.

Tommy was a salesman and a farmer. He had a way about him. On one occasion when the social worker was initiating a conversation on Tommy's perspective of his end of life, he turned the tables on her. As an excellent salesman, he knew how to answer a question with a question. "Where are you going to spend eternity?" he asked. He totally caught her off guard.

I thought of the Lord's Prayer. (See Matthew 6:9-13 KJV.) The promised "for ever" has no limit, no expiration date, no boundaries. Our decisions today guarantee our forever existence. We must lift up our cup of salvation and make it available to everyone (Psalm 116:13 NLT).

"Until death do us part." The vows spoken in love bound Tommy and I. Had we fought the good fight, finished the race to God's glory? We had disappointed each other and our Father many times. We had argued, withheld love and respect. Unity was not always our focus. But we did persevere through God's unfailing and unconditional love, strength, and courage. Today, I continue to pray that our perseverance testified to the faith we had in God and each other — that forever kind of love.

We tuned the page and focused on the whole body. Tommy was moved to inpatient Hospice; palliative measures were the priority. The view became heavenward, God's beautiful palette. *"We know that if our earthly tent we live in is destroyed, we have a building from God, an eternal dwelling in the heavens, not made with hands"* (2 Corinthians 5:1 CSB).

With my whole heart, I was seeking my Father God. I needed my wonderful Counselor! My mind was pounding to know the truth, to be able to decide what was best for Tommy, to not be ashamed, bearing no reproach or contempt. I was burdened, trampled in the dust of confusion. I prayed Psalm 143:8: *"Let me experience your faithful love in the morning, for I trust in you. Reveal to me the way I should go because I appeal to you"* (CSB).

Though Tommy was not communicating, I felt he surely was experiencing Psalm 119:81-88.

Psalm 119 was my mantra during those twelve, long weeks. As I meditated, prayed, and pleaded, a wise nurse consulted with the physician for pain control methods, which would allow Tommy to go home for his last days.

"In my distress I called to the Lord and he answered me" (Psalm 120:1 csb).

The pages were now flipping swiftly, and I was very grateful for my Father's presence and our children's constant attention. *"Yea, though I walk through the valley of the shadow of death, I will fear no evil: for thou art with me; thy rod and thy staff they comfort me"* (Psalm 23:4 kjv).

The words on the pages were blurred as if I were speed reading to the end. Was this God's mercy? Mercy comes in different forms for those experiencing the need. God, in his wisdom, knew Tommy's need for mercy. His grace tempered our cups filled with hot grief so we could taste His goodness and mercy.

We were not going home. I grieved, "Will I ever hear his voice again or see his eyes open?"

My husband worked hard to stay alive for us, but it was his time. Several days earlier he had cried, "I can't take care of my family." I had warned him that he was overloading his body with physical and mental labor. Did he finally understand my love and fear in those warnings? I pray he did.

As he struggled to breathe, we gathered around the bed, my son prayed, and my son-in-law sang "Hallelujah." God's angels flew through the heavens and gathered Tommy at 8:28 p.m. est on July 10, 2018. The Great Physician gathered him in His arms, cleansed him from all disease, and freed him from pain. The last tale had been told; the last chapter had been lived.

22

Lessons Learned from Covid-19 Through the Cross

Ginny Dent Brant

When will life return to normal? We may never return to the way things used to be. We will face a new normal with lessons learned from this pandemic. Germs, bacteria and viruses have been around since the Fall of Man, but we are much more aware of them than before. So, what might those lessons be?

- We are now more cognizant of ways germs and bacteria spread. We'll be washing our hands more often, longer, and more thoroughly in an attempt to prevent any flu or virus from spreading. We may decide to use a glove each time we pump gas into our cars, knowing that germs and viruses from many people are lingering on that nozzle. I know I'll never go to the grocery store without wiping down my cart handle with sanitizer. And if I'm sick, I'll do everyone a favor and stay home! Do unto others as you would have them do unto you. Or simply stated: Treat others the way you want to be treated.

- We'll probably never look at our children's teachers the same. Instead of, "I know my child would never do that!" It'll be, "Bless you teacher, and how may I work with you?" Some parents may decide to continue home schooling. And some, for fear of what might happen if schools never re-opened, will have them at school on time if not early. Parents may now understand the previous notes the teacher sent home. We as parents are the first and most important teachers of our children. May we teach and model for them the values that Jesus lived.

- We might designate one closet or space storing extra sanitizer, toilet paper, paper towels, gloves, masks, and nonperishable food. We'll never forget the day when a roll of toilet paper was more valuable than a gallon of gas. But what's even more valuable is the fact that because of Christ's redeeming work on The Cross, my sins are paid in full. That is of immeasurable value! As Dr. Sandy Stradtman said, "The sin 'virus' is much more pervasive and deadly, as we know. The Coronavirus is something we can catch; sin determines who we are at the heart level. The death rate from Coronavirus is about three percent or less; the death rate from sin is one-hundred percent."

- We realize that our days on earth are at best . . . tenuous and temporary. Only what's done for Christ will matter. In Heaven, there will be no more sickness, germs or bacteria. Keeping this eternal perspective keeps us sane when everything around us appears to be bordering on insanity. No matter what kind of quarantine we are under, God can't be contained in a box. He can't be quarantined. He is holy! He's always with us. Nothing has changed. Sickness, germs and bacteria will ultimately be defeated for good.

- God uses suffering to get our attention. He wants us to look to Him for strength; to look within to see what we need changing; to look around and see how we can make a difference in this world. We won't forget those folks who went all out to provide PPE, ventilators, and other critical needs. People donating and making things they'd never made before to meet an urgent need is the heart of America. And the message of the church continues to reach the world through creative means. Who'd ever have thought Samaritan's Purse would set up a mobile medical unit in Central Park! Our gratitude for The Cross motivates us to reach out to others.

- We'll never take for granted those who served on the frontlines — doctors, nurses, military, first responders, delivery personnel, grocers, etc. They either saved people's lives or helped keep our economy and essentials moving. The message of The Cross teaches us that the greatest act on this earth is to give your life for others.

- We now know that our immune systems are front and center in defending us against any flu or virus. In addition to CDC recommendations, we must also keep hydrated, keep moving, get adequate rest, eat immunity-building foods, and eat probiotic foods to keep our gut and immune systems armed and ready for battle. Many doctors and nutritionists will tell you that keeping your immune system strong in addition to social distancing, washing hands, and isolating those who are ill is critical. In addition to age, it was underlying conditions such as heart disease, diabetes, asthma and chronic lung issues — some of which were caused by our own lifestyle habits — that made Covid-19 more aggressive in some than others. Our responsibility to care for our bodies becomes more important every day. God has gifted us with an amazing body that is armed and ready for combat when we treat it responsibly.

- Our trust in the Chinese government may and should be limited. Their cover-up of the truth cost the entire world much. It will be difficult to trust their leaders. (This does not apply to our Chinese-American citizens.) As a result, we may be making more things here in the good ole USA — especially our cherished pharmaceuticals and medical supplies! Let's quit looking for people to blame. China and their delay and cover-up are to blame. If intentional, the world must deal with China's leaders. But if by accident, we must show mercy. God has forgiven us through The Cross. Might we forgive others?

We have far more going our way than those who lived and died during the Spanish Flu epidemic in 1918-1919. Medical technology, ventilators and drugs, including antibiotics, were unavailable when this pandemic swept through the world infecting five-hundred-million and killing up to fifty-million people. And they did not have the Internet to keep schools, businesses, and communication up and running. We do best when we learn from the lessons we've learned during Covid-19 through the lens of The Cross.

May this pandemic be an awakening that leads us back to The Cross of Christ. We have much to be thankful for in the eye of this pandemic. So what are you thankful for? I'm thankful for my health, family — especially my two grandsons born healthy during this pandemic — and that in the New Heaven and Earth germs, bacteria, and viruses will be obliterated.

23

A Hero's Hope

Erma M. Ullrey

Morning sun streaked through the windows on June 20, 2017. Bert and I looked around our familiar farmhouse then closed the door for the last time. Lingering on the porch we gazed out over the small Christmas tree farm we'd cultivated, then sighed in admiration of our gorgeous Mt. Adams view. Chickens pecked and neighbors waved as we drove away, leaving our three acres, four adult children, and two grandchildren to spend our golden years in the beautiful Boise, Idaho area.

A few months prior, Bert had experienced some bleeding causing him to visit our nurse practitioner. At age fifty-nine, this was the first time he'd been advised to get a colonoscopy. With the move a few short weeks away, he opted to wait until we transitioned to our new home.

After we settled, long-time friends invited us to attend their local church in Idaho. We fell in love with the pastor and people, and joined one of their small fellowship groups. Everyone in the group treated us like family, and we enjoyed their warmth every Tuesday night.

Bert established with a new primary care doctor in August, then secured a colonoscopy appointment for September.

Colorectal cancer. As the gastroenterologist gently delivered the diagnosis, Bert's breathing quickened. My heart pounded like a thundering drum that drowned out the dreaded words.

There had to be some mistake. For the first time in decades, it was only the two of us, beginning a new adventure. But now the golden years looked more like a dark abyss.

Dr. O, a colorectal surgeon, scheduled a few more tests. As Bert prepped for a CT, he told the technician, "I guess this is serious."

It was. PET scan and MRI revealed colon cancer, three cancerous lesions in his liver, and an unidentified lesion in his right lung. The news shattered our world: Stage 4A colorectal cancer, metastatic to the liver and lung.

Given these findings, Bert was not a surgical candidate. We learned that due to the placement of his liver cancer, he wasn't a candidate for radiation either. And because of his bleeding, Bert could only receive two of the three recommended chemotherapy drugs. Rather than curative therapy, the goal was palliative. In other words, they'd hope for the best but. . . . The unspoken words echoed certain hopelessness.

In these surreal moments, Bert's stoic nature shone. Because of our medical background, Bert understood the terminology and grasped every word the doctor said, as well as those he hadn't. Yet he chose to cling to the Lord.

We prayed that the Lord would heal Bert completely. Everyone we knew prayed for healing as well. We knew God always answers prayers, but we weren't sure He'd give the answer we wanted.

A few months earlier, on a sweltering August day, we'd begun to think about Christmas. Specifically, Christmas concerts. Turns out, it was the first day we could buy tickets for the Amy Grant/Michael W. Smith concert in our area. We scooped up tickets for us and three friends. The date of the concert was Wednesday, November 15th, ironically, the day Bert's chemo treatments would begin.

We arrived early to the hospital that morning for the first treatment. Our nurse, Alice, spent the morning supplying as much information as our brains could hold. With grace and patience, she answered all our questions. When we told her about our concert plans that evening, she was jealous. She'd tried to buy tickets but she was too late.

It began to rain late that afternoon but we parked close and ran to the security check-point. Bert had attached his chemotherapy infusion pump, a medicine-filled cylinder inside a bright blue vinyl sleeve, through a belt loop on his pants. A security officer took him aside and asked about the "torpedo," as Bert affectionately called it. As he began his explanation, the officer's eyes grew wide. He jumped back and asked Bert to hurry inside. The look on the officer's face was the humor we needed at that moment.

The concert was amazing from start to finish. But, when Jordan Smith began to sing, "All Is Well," a flood-gate of long-harnessed emotions opened and crashed against the Almighty's throne.

My husband and best friend of thirty-seven years, my children's father, my grandchildren's papa, had inoperable Stage 4 cancer. I shouldn't have, but I'd checked online. The cure rate for this type of cancer was 14%. Jordan's strong, silky voice continued heralding *All Is Well*. I bristled. How is it well? What's *well* about cancer?

I looked over at Bert. Unlike me, he wasn't crying or cowering. His grin stretched from ear to ear while he soaked up every note. Despite his death sentence, he'd chosen to enjoy the moments. Given his example, how could I do less?

On Valentine's Day 2018, Bert's blood CEA measured 2.2. After this seventh treatment, the oncologist would schedule a CT to determine the effectiveness of the chemo drugs. We walked on clouds of joy toward our bay where we'd once again sit with chemotherapy coursing through Bert's body.

I'd forgotten to silence my phone that morning, but it didn't matter. My iPad flashed the words "missed calls" from our youngest daughter. As unusual as it was to get a call from her during work hours, it was equally unusual to receive calls in the basement of the hospital. We later learned, unusual would fill our day.

I left Bert, who slept peacefully in a soft recliner, and returned our daughter's call. I was told a car traveling twenty miles per hour had struck our oldest daughter, a nurse.

She had been thrown into the air and hit her head when she landed on the slick pavement. MRI and x-rays showed no internal injuries, broken bones, or sprains. They later diagnosed her with a concussion. She suffered severe headaches, significant pain, and vivid nightmares during the weeks that followed. She told us that as she flew through the air, she saw the blue sky and knew angels surrounded her.

How does someone get hit by a car, yet survive as beautifully as our daughter did? Our praise continues to rise to the Lord for His hand of protection and mercy.

The Tumor Board met regarding Bert's case. On our return visit, the oncologist burst into a small waiting room, all smiles, and announced, "My chemo works." Bert and I looked at each other and responded, "Yes, and our God heals."

As the oncologist placed Bert's scans from October 2017 alongside the scans from February 2018, we could see what God had done. The bright red areas that delineated cancer no longer appeared. We sat speechless, consumed with awe.

So often we cried out to Jesus repeating His words *by His stripes we are healed.* Humbled by the healing touch of our Savior, inadequate, unending words of praise spilled out.

Bert had surgery on March 15th. After a four-day hospital stay, he returned home without a colostomy or an ileostomy. Pathology showed zero out of twenty-two lymph nodes affected by cancer.

God healed Bert! There is no other explanation.

At Bert's six-week post-op visit, Dr. O said something interesting. "We don't like to use the word *cured,* but. . . ."

Unlike Dr. O, we have no problem with the word cured because that's exactly what God did.

24

The Challenges of Caregiving

Norma C. Mezoe

"What!" I screeched.

The morning had been stressful from beginning to ending.

Gene, my husband, seldom comes into the kitchen except for meals, so when I heard him coming, I was expecting negative talk and I got it.

"Who's doing all of that loud talking!"

Up until this time, the kitchen had been quiet. I was doing my devotional and Bible reading, which I try to do before Gene arises.

He wasn't wearing his hearing aid and could not understand when I tried to explain no one was talking. He angrily grabbed his walker and shuffled back to the living room. Showing his frustration, he gave the walker a hard shove, knocking it onto the floor.

I put his hearing aid in and when I did, the loud talking went away, according to Gene. He has Alzheimer's Disease and one of the side effects in the more advanced stage is hallucinations. Three times before, he had heard a man singing loudly and yelled for me to turn off the radio. The house had been quiet during those times also.

When I asked what he wanted for breakfast, he said he wasn't hungry. Later, he changed his mind and ordered a large meal of sausage, scrambled eggs, gravy, and fried potatoes. Although earlier he had said he wanted orange juice he was now upset and complained that he had told me three times he wanted tomato juice.

By the time his breakfast ended and he'd expressed other complaints, I was tired from the stress. He finally made his way back to his recliner and I had the kitchen to myself.

In a short while, he yelled at me.

Assuming it was going to be another demand or complaint, that was when I screeched, "What!"

Imagine my emotions when he quietly said, "I just want to thank you for my good breakfast."

From having watched my father care for my mother, I am aware caregivers face many challenges in meeting the needs of family members dealing with various forms of mental and physical illness. Often, they go without needed sleep in order to provide the care necessary for loved ones. Many times they eat meals on the run.

For twelve years, my elderly father faced many obstacles as he took care of the needs of my mother who suffered with several illnesses, including Alzheimer's.

As Dad learned the facets of being a caregiver, he assumed many of the duties Mom had been responsible for in the past. He cooked, washed dishes, did laundry, and grocery shopped. I tried to help as much as possible, but most of the caregiving was on Dad's shoulders.

Mom's personality had always been gentle, but on at least one occasion she showed a completely different side. Dad had been trying to get her to do something she didn't want to do.

She looked at him with frustration and then declared loudly, "I wish you would die!"

I watched as Dad wilted and held back tears. Mom would never have spoken those words before her illness.

It seems to be a well-known fact that patients with Alzheimer's and other forms of dementia take their frustrations and anger out on their caregivers, who often are family members. This is what Dad learned and what I am now learning.

If you would like to assist caregivers, there are a number of ways to lend a helping hand and offer encouragement — things such as phoning the caregiver and allowing them to share frustrations, sending cards and letters, or offering to stay with the patient so the caregiver can grocery shop, make doctor's appointments, or have lunch with a friend.

It also helps the caregiver to know that people are thinking about and praying for them and the patient.

I am aware friends and family are praying for Gene and for me. I have the assurance of their love as well as knowing God's love surrounds us every moment.

I know there will be more challenges and other difficult decisions to make in the future. Verses such as Psalm 46:1, *God is our refuge and strength, an ever present help in trouble* (NIV), offer reminders that I will not have to face them alone.

That assurance offers peace beyond human understanding.

25

Through It All

Diana Derringer

*Rejoice with those who rejoice;
mourn with those who mourn.*

Romans 12:15 NIV

The world stopped
along with my husband's heart.

With one call to our church,
support appeared at the hospital
even before we arrived.
Waiting, praying, feeding,
holding, crying,
they came unobtrusively,
lovingly offering anything we might be needing.
They mourned with me
At the frailty of life.

Twenty-four hours later,
he breathed on his own,
and spoke with a squeeze of his hand.
They continued to come
waiting, praying, feeding,
holding, crying,
they came unobtrusively,
lovingly offering anything we might be needing.
They rejoiced with me
In the miracle of life.

26

Cancer and Chrysanthemums

April Pope

The yellow mums were fading fast, but they had been too pretty to dump in the woods this year. I always felt guilty about taking my ferns and other seasonal plants to the horticultural graveyard below our pond. I had bought these mums at the local grocery store, and for the last few weeks they, along with pumpkins and cornstalks, announced to everyone who drove past our farmhouse, "It's fall, Ya'll." I decided that next weekend would be liberation day for these yellow beauties, and that I would plant them in the bed in front of the house where they would be our harbingers of fall forever.

Then the pain started. Not severe, but persistent pain, like a toothache. I used words like mild, dull, and achy to describe the pain in my left breast to my physician. "At least cancer doesn't hurt," the mammography tech said. "Your last mammogram was only eight months ago and it was normal, so I'm sure it's nothing."

Thirty minutes later, she walked back in the room, and I remember thinking that she would make a terrible poker player. With a scripted tone, she said, "The radiologist saw something, so we need to head over to the ultrasound room."

That was the beginning of my cancer journey.

On October 25th I had the biopsy. On October 28th I got the phone call from my surgeon, "You have invasive ductal carcinoma of the left breast." On October 31st my husband and I sat at a large conference table and the surgeon explained, "You have a very aggressive form of breast cancer that often does not have a good prognosis. But it looks like we found it early."

Yay me!

On November 4th I had a mastectomy, and I was scheduled to start an aggressive regimen of chemo that would last sixteen weeks, beginning on December 4th.

Merry Christmas to me.

Priorities — how quickly they can be realigned. Just six weeks earlier I had thought I was healthy. My biggest concern had been switching seasonal cornstalks for jack-o-lanterns, and feeling guilty about not getting plants in the ground before the first frost of the year.

Now I wondered if I would be alive at Christmas. Strangely enough, I could not stop worrying about my mums. My poor mums were all but dead at this point. Between MRIs, blood work, port placements, oncology appointments, and surgery, the plants were not high on my priority list. As I looked at my dying mums, I couldn't help but wonder if I was dying too? I wondered if this plant would make it through the long winter. I wondered the same thing about me. Would either of us emerge in the spring when our dormant period of hibernation was over? If we did make it, would we ever blossom again?

I learned many lessons through my cancer trial. The first lesson was for me to do my part, and to let God do His part. So, two weeks after my mastectomy I did my part and I planted the mums. Now it was up to God to do His part. Only God can make things live or die, and no amount of stress or worry will ever change that.

That was lesson number two.

The stranger in the mirror resembled me, sort of. I remember laughing out loud in my bathroom as I thought, *the very hairs on my head are numbered by the Lord.* "Well God, at least your job is a lot easier now." Then, I thought about my mums. They too were withered externally, but I prayed that the roots were still alive.

What about me? Was the old me still in there somewhere? Would the old me flush back out and be able to return to life as I knew it before?

I counted down the days, and finally the day that I had waited for arrived. My last treatment was completed on March 11th and spring was in the air. Anxiously, I waited for signs of life, both in the mirror and in the soil.

One sunny morning, it happened. Tender, green shoots had emerged overnight from deep beneath the earth. This time, the green leaves were not the harbingers of fall, they were harbingers of hope. Tears streamed down my face as I thanked God for allowing new life, both for my mums and for me. God had done His part, just as He promised He would and I knew that I was going to be okay.

Although dormancy is necessary for perennial plants to grow, we don't think about dormancy for ourselves as Christians. One definition describes dormancy as having normal functions slowed down for a period of time. I can testify that being forced to slow down allowed me to grow spiritually. The roots of my faith in Christ grew deeper, and for that I will forever be grateful. I learned the hard lesson that we must trust God when we cannot see what lies beneath the soil of our life.

Romans 8:28 (KJV) tells us *we know that all things work together for good to them that love God, to them who are the called according to his purpose.*

We do not know what God has planned for our lives, but we can know that even when things are bad, He can use them for good. Each year my chrysanthemum "dies" but each year it grows back bigger and more beautiful than it was the previous year. Thanks to my period of dormancy, I now have a closer relationship with Christ.

If you are going through a trial right now, use the opportunity to grow your faith. If God works in the dark recesses of the cold earth, to bring life to a plant, don't you think that he will work for us even on our darkest days?

> *Thank you Father for loving us enough to allow us to grow through our trials. Help us remember that when all we see is withered stems you are working on the beautiful flowers that will emerge when our winter is over.*

27

The Journey that Doesn't Make Sense

Debbie Presnell

I couldn't have imagined that six months after responding to God's call to write and teach a Bible study on joy while suffering, I'd be writing it from the 3rd floor of an oncology center. My exploration through the book of James was about to get real.

Yep. Cancer.

Like an uninvited hitchhiker, cancer burst onto the path of my husband, Alan, and thus my own journey.

We were certainly blindsided by our medical emergency, but we had to put our heads together, become proactive, and deal with the unthinkable — this unexpected, unforeseen, distraction . . . the epitome of evil.

A nurse advised, "Clear your calendar. You're going to be busy." So, I did. And while my body was physically on the move, my mind began to quietly wonder.

I wondered about many things. *When You, God, told me to write a Bible study on joy during suffering, was it to prepare me for this sickness? Or will this sickness prepare me to write from the perspective of authentic experience?* But it didn't matter which came first. They were both here.

What I fearfully wondered was how I would manage without him.

I wondered how I would focus on the essentials of managing a home and helping my three adult children trust God about their Dad's illness, and not become angry or question God's plan.

I wondered how I would work — as a teacher, speaker, or writer.

I wondered about the lessons I fully expected would come.

I wondered if I would stay strong . . . and would my husband, too?

I wondered about a lot of things while trying to encourage my husband and continue to be the "Pollyanna" he'd always known me to be.

So, I focused on Alan, his needs, the Bible, and prayer. As a Christ-follower, I grasped that this cancer was not unexpected by God. It had been carefully sifted through His hands. I knew God had always been and would continue to be faithful.

But then, an unpredictable and astonishing thought popped into my head, and deeply touched my heart.

Yes, popped! A deliberate thought, placed there by God. He was again calling me to action. He whispered to my heart. *I'm not asking for your permission to change your journey. I've been faithful to you. Will you remain faithful to me?*

Faithful.

"Yes, I *want* to do that," I said aloud.

But then I wondered again. *What could it mean for me to be faithful to Him?*

As the weeks progressed, the autumn leaves fell in heaps on the ground. Our adult children gathered to rake and bag them for us. A grandson was born. Soon, the cold winter winds began to blow.

Most days were spent at one doctor's office or another getting an infusion, surgery checkups, PET scans, and the like. But all days were spent in prayer, reading the Bible, and with Alan and I talking together about the observations and responses we'd seen from each other, the people who love us, and for the many people who were praying.

And then it happened.

I heard the most surprising and beautiful words I had ever heard. Alan and I were sitting on the sofa watching TV when he reached over to me, touched my hand and said, "I have something to say."

"Okay," I said inquisitively.

"I have so much joy right now," he said. "I guess this doesn't make sense coming from a man with cancer." He chuckled. "But I do. In fact, I may have the most joy I've ever had in my whole life."

Tears filled my eyes and gently coursed down my face.

"When they show I'm cancer free, I'll fall prostrate on the floor and praise God. Well, regardless of what happens . . . I'll fall prostrate and praise God."

That's when we both knew we were living the life that doesn't make sense, humanly speaking. It doesn't make sense to be simultaneously sad and joyful — sad that my husband was suffering the side effects and pain of cancer, yet joyful at the magnitude of God's blessings while in it. We were walking with God, drowning in His grace, and experiencing the blessing of laughter and internal change.

James 1:2 came alive for me. *Consider it pure joy, my brothers and sisters, whenever you face trials of many kinds.* (NIV)

Then I understood.

The trial in and of itself doesn't produce joy; rather, joy flows from the realization that God has us both — our entire family — in His grip and He will never let us go. The joy comes in knowing we're never out of His thoughts. Joy arises in the transformation we recognize in ourselves and in others.

This. This, then, is what I've come to love — the journey that doesn't make sense.

It doesn't make sense to suddenly become brave, but in hard times, we did. I was reminded of a quote from JD Greear that I've learned to love: God doesn't call the brave; He makes brave those He calls.

It doesn't make sense at 6:30 A.M. during a torrential downpour that Alan, without complaining, strapped on a knee brace to relieve the pain so he could fulfill his work commitment and provide for our future.

It doesn't make sense that while the doctors were preparing to do

MRI to see if the cancer had spread to his brain, Alan, smiling, said he felt peaceful.

And it doesn't make sense that my husband would tell me to go fulfill my purpose by serving the women in India while he needed me to serve him. "I don't want to give the devil that satisfaction," he said.

Hugging me he said, "I'm glad it's me." No. From my perspective, this *absolutely makes no sense.*

* * *

Maybe it's a confusing time and you just need this reminder to trust that God will do what doesn't make sense if you remain faithful to Him.

So, about that. *How do we remain faithful?*

To be faithful to God means

- we give our steadfast devotion to Him alone. We refuse to look to another person or situation. Proverbs 4:27 warns, *Do not turn to the right nor the left.* Psalm 107:9 reminds us our thirst will never be satisfied with what the world has to offer. Only God satisfies the thirsty.
- there's joy amid the sadness. Happiness is based on emotions and wavers as our situation does. Joy comes from standing on God's word and believing He has a plan.
- we expect His strength for every task we deal with and each emotion that floods the heart. Nehemiah 8:10 tells us *the joy of the Lord is your strength.*
- we spend time reading His Word. Jeremiah wrote this: *Your words were found and I ate them. And Your words became for me a joy and the delight of the heart* (Jeremiah 15:16).
- we wait in hopeful expectation. Romans 12:12 tells us to *rejoice in our confident hope. Be patient in trouble, and keep on praying.*

When we are faithful to God, we can expect the unexpected and experience joy in the journey that doesn't make sense.

28

The Enemy Within

Marian Rizzo

It began with a sore throat. No big deal, I've had them before. Sometimes from a simple allergy, sometimes from a cold or a virus. You gargle with saltwater, suck on a lozenge, and eventually it goes away.

But this sore throat didn't go away. Within a couple of days, I had a fever. Okay, so it wasn't a simple allergy. Maybe the flu. I took Tylenol and the fever came down a little. It didn't go away completely. Soon, I experienced the worst chills I'd ever had. I wrapped myself in a heavy quilt and sat in my recliner — for hours — watching TV, flipping through channels, reading a book, reciting Scriptures. . . . whatever I could do to keep my mind off my misery.

I lost my appetite, went through several days with recurring nausea. During that time I lost seven pounds, not a major problem because I'd been trying to lose twenty.

My doctor put me on a Z-pack and Zinc. I started eating again and gained back the seven pounds, plus two more.

Still, things didn't seem right. I suffered from shortness of breath. A walk to the mailbox at the end of my driveway left me panting for air. I couldn't take a deep breath, you know the kind, when you've inflated your lungs to the fullest. That lasted for a couple of weeks, but gradually, almost imperceptibly, my breathing got better.

I went for long walks, inhaled the fresh morning air, talked to God and thanked Him for helping me breathe normally again.

But was I really free? Other annoyances began to surface. Pain on the bottoms of my feet flared up, like they were on fire. Even before I got out of bed I felt as if I'd been walking on hot coals. The big toes on both of my feet throbbed with pain. My podiatrist diagnosed the symptoms as poor circulation. He recommended compression hose. I bought two pair at twenty dollars each. They didn't make any difference. I put them in a drawer, took Ibuprofen, and went about my day.

Within a couple of weeks, the burning sensation subsided. But a short time after that, the second toe on my right foot began to change shape. It turned purple and throbbed with intense pain. My daughter showed me a site on the internet.

"You've got 'Covid toe,' " she told me.

I peered at the images. Sure enough, they looked exactly like my toe. It was as if someone had snuck inside my house with a camera and photographed my foot when I wasn't looking.

All along I'd been suspecting that I had contracted Covid-19, though I was never tested. I decided to go for a blood test and find out if I had the antibodies in my system. I waited too long. The blood test needs to be done within a few weeks of being sick.

Five months have passed since I got the sore throat and fever. Yet, every now and then I feel flushed. Or I get another sore throat that lasts maybe a day or just a couple of hours. Or I endure another bout of chills. Or my feet burn. Sometimes, I have trouble taking a deep breath. I even got an unexpected toothache.

The truth is, what if I only thought I'd been cured? What if the virus never left my body at all but surfaces now and then in different manifestations? What if it has taken up permanent residence inside me and is still at work, attacking, slowly destroying me on the inside?

Corona virus didn't act like any other virus. It seems to have a mind of its own, like it can think and plot and attack at will.

What will it take to completely annihilate this insidious beast? I can think of only one great mind that could wipe it out completely. The Creator Who made the world and everything in it, Who knows everything, including the workings of a virus — He is the one who can flush the monster from my body and make me whole again.

And so I turn to the Scriptures. I recite Psalm 121, *I will lift up mine eyes unto the hills, from whence cometh my help* (KJV). The Psalmist goes on to say that help comes from the Lord, who will not suffer my foot to be moved, who never slumbers; who is the shade upon my right hand; who never allows the sun to smite me by day or the moon by night, and who preserves my going out and coming in forevermore.

I also consider the words of Job: *The Lord gave and the Lord hath taken away; blessed be the name of the Lord* (1:21 KJV) and *Though He slay me, yet will I trust in Him* (13:15 KJV). A certain spiritual strength accompanies that kind of recitation. It isn't a form of giving up. Rather, it's victory, because I've put the problem at His feet and left it there. Of course, I'll continue to watch for a cure. I'll take note of the symptoms that occur over time.

I may never be free of the effects of this virus. It could surface over and over again throughout the rest of my life, maliciously attacking when least expected, tearing my body down, piece by piece, like mini sniper attacks. But this unseen enemy cannot touch my soul. It cannot weaken my faith in God, cannot crush my spirit. In the end, I will win. I know I will, not because I'm so strong and capable, but because my Redeemer is. He lives and He holds me in the palm of His hand.

29

Embrace the Fleeting Days

Ann Brubaker Greenleaf Wirtz

My husband, Arie, thought he'd torn the deltoid muscle in his left arm when he pulled on a frozen hangar door at the Lakeland Airport in Northern Wisconsin. He was checking on his VariEze experimental aircraft when the incident occurred. Although no x-rays were ever taken, a doctor agreed it was a tear. It would heal on its own.

Eight months later we were in western North Carolina, living in a charming, cranberry-colored, cottage-style house on the side of Davis Mountain. The breathtaking grandeur and warmer clime of the southern Blue Ridge had called us. After thirty-five years of marriage and more than twenty moves, we declared this was our permanent home until heaven.

During this time, Arie's arm never healed and even grew larger. Despite the increasing discomfort, we never thought the problem was anything more than a muscle tear. We were in our new home another eight months when it became obvious the tear wasn't healing on its own and surgery seemed the only solution. An appointment with an orthopedic surgeon was scheduled.

Our thirty-sixth wedding anniversary was only weeks away in August 2003, as we patiently sat in the doctor's office waiting for the MRI results. Striding into the room, Dr. Brooks attached the x-rays to the lighted screen and said softly, "This is cancer."

Stunned, we leapt from our seats to peer at the black and white image, trying to comprehend the tumor shadowing his muscle.

Backing away in horror, I sank into my chair, staring in disbelief. I whispered, "Are you sure?"

"I'm as sure of this as I am of my grandmother," he replied firmly, explaining he would send Arie to see Dr. John Eady at the University of South Carolina School of Medicine in Columbia. He added, "I'm a Duke man, but Dr. Eady is the best in the southeast to handle your problem. He's head of the Orthopedic Surgery Department and specializes in tumors in the arm and shoulder."

Dr. Brooks left the room to make arrangements, and I immediately went to Arie. We held each other, shocked and trembling at this incomprehensible news.

"I'm so sorry! I'm so sorry," he cried.

"No, Darling, don't be sorry!" I pleaded. "I'm so sorry for YOU!"

We were clueless about what lay ahead but were determined to trust and cling to the Lord, no matter what happened, knowing He would be with us. As we embarked on this unknown journey, we wanted faith to be at the forefront of every step and every decision. The Bible verse Deuteronomy 33:27 (NLT) immediately came to mind to calm and encourage our fearful hearts: *The eternal God is your refuge, and underneath are the everlasting arms.*

Sleep was elusive that long, first night. Out of the depths of my agony, I could only muster two prayers, "Dear Father, help us I pray; keep us safe by night and day!" and "Help us, Jesus!" I was God's child offering the simplest of prayers, and the repetition kept the darkest fears at bay.

The following week, we sat in Dr. Eady's office waiting for his interpretation of the test results. Our packed suitcases were in the car, and we had put out extra cat food for Willow. We figured we'd be gone several days while Arie was in the hospital having the tumor removed. (Oh, yes, we were clueless.)

Instead, Dr. Eady explained succinctly, "This is a soft tissue cancer, a sarcoma, Malignant Fibrous Histiocytoma (MFH). You'll have chemotherapy to reduce the size of the tumor, and if we get a clear margin, then we'll operate to remove it. You'll probably lose your arm, but our goal is to save your life."

Following that astonishing pronouncement, we drove two hours and one-hundred thirty-six miles back home to Hendersonville, North Carolina, suitcases unopened, a trip filling us with even more disbelief, dread and uncertainty.

Four rounds of five-day, in-hospital chemotherapy ensued, and after three months Dr. Eady was able to manipulate the tumor in Arie's arm. He declared it had shrunk enough for surgery, although the scan showed the margin was thin, at best. Three days before Christmas, Dr. Eady was still in his scrubs when he called us into a private room and showed us the tumor. We were dumbfounded to see it was the size of a small grapefruit!

Weeks of daily radiation followed recovery. When a routine CT scan revealed the cancer had metastasized to Arie's lungs, radiation was done. We opted for more rounds of chemotherapy, but in late May when the scans came back showing increased tumor growth, we knew we had lost the battle. We signed up for Hospice, grateful for this blessed organization and thankful for all who'd helped us along the way. Forever dear would be our oncologist, Dr. James E. Radford, Jr., who came to the Hospice home, the Elizabeth House, to see us the day my husband entered in early July 2004.

Twelve days later, Arie died. He had just turned sixty-five. Looking back, the journey proved to be more than a battle with cancer. It proved an instructor of life. Arie's cancer revealed multiple truths:

- Life is fragile and over quickly, regardless of the number of years lived.
- We should cherish each day and each person, especially beloved family and dear friends.
- Accepting and embracing faith in Jesus Christ is the most important and eternal reality of life.

- We can rejoice in the Lord through scripture reading, prayer, and praise.
- We should express gratitude and forgiveness.
- We need to value the days of illness, they give us time to love.
- We should embrace the truth of heaven, home for the believer whose salvation is in Christ Jesus, and share this Good News with others.

We experienced the truth of heaven when Arie died at 5:50 A.M. With tears and a kiss good-bye, the finality of his death hard to comprehend, I called our son Arie Todd. He and his wife Dewa were living an hour away in Greenville, South Carolina. He answered immediately and shared the following:

> I woke at 5:45 and the apartment was very cold. I got up and fixed the air conditioner then sat on the side of the bed and drank some water. The clock read 5:49. I was wondering if Dad had died in the night. Suddenly, I was aware of his voice softly within me, filled with emotion, a sense of wonderment, excitement, and at the same time his voice quality and tone held total peace and assurance.
>
> Dad said, "O, Todd, it's so glorious, more glorious than you can ever imagine!"
>
> I lay back down thinking this is what Dad would say if he could. Two or three minutes later the phone rang, and I knew it was Mom calling to tell me he had died.

This glimpse of glory was and is a gift to our family and is shared to bring hope and comfort to others in the journey. Cancer brings fear and sorrow. Yet, in a fascinating way, it also gives us a gift, the gift of time to leave nothing of faith or love unsaid, if we but embrace the fleeting days.

30

What's My Number?

Lydia E. Harris

Your eyes saw my unformed body; all the days ordained for me were written in your book before one of them came to be. How precious to me are your thoughts, God!

Psalm 139:16–17 NIV

Tears filled my eyes as I stared blankly out the kitchen window. My heart felt heavy. The doctor's words that afternoon were not what I wanted to hear. "Studies show the prognosis for your type of cancer is not good."

Waves of fear washed over me as the doctor's dismal words replayed in my mind. "Your prognosis is not as good . . . not as good . . . not as good." What did his words mean — exactly? Not as good as what? I didn't think *anything* about cancer was good. Now my illness sounded worse than I expected. Bleak thoughts swirled around me. What would happen to me? How would this disease progress? Would my life now be filled with one bad report after another?

An inner voice interrupted my churning questions. "This medical report hasn't changed anything, Lydia."

What was that?

"You are still going to live every day I planned for you."

I wiped my eyes, startled by this unexpected revelation. Was God speaking to me?

The encouraging words continued. "I don't want you on an emotional roller-coaster, going up and down every time you hear good or bad news."

That sounded reassuring. I didn't like roller-coaster emotions either.

"You will receive varying medical reports. But they won't change the length of your life. The doctors haven't numbered your days. I have. The end is fixed. The ups and downs in between will not shorten your life."

I dried my tears and pondered these words. Wasn't there a Bible passage that said something about God numbering our days? I turned to Psalm 139, a chapter I had read many times over the years. Now verse 16 took on new meaning. *Your eyes saw my unformed body. All the days ordained for me were written in your book before one of them came to be."*

I knew God had ordained the length of my life long before I was born, but for the first time, I realized my illness could *not* shorten their number. I would still live *every* day God had planned for me.

Reassuring ripples of hope filled my heart, and God's comforting peace poured in. God had a loving plan for each day of my life — and nothing could change how many days he had ordained for me. *"How precious to me are your thoughts, O God!"* (Psalm 139:17 NIV).

As I continue my journey with cancer and the ups and downs it brings, I keep reminding myself of this crucial truth: Illness has not shortened my life.

Health challenges or other adverse circumstances cannot shorten your life either. We don't know the specific number of days God has planned for each of us, but we don't need to. God is in control. We can trust Him. Our responsibility lies in how we spend each day, with God's help. Let's purpose to view every moment as a gift from God, to live fully for his glory. Then, no matter the number of our days, each one will count for God.

31
Laughing with God

Esther M. Bailey

When I started chemotherapy, I thought I was prepared for my loss of hair. I had even quipped to my husband, "Maybe I'll get rid of my dandruff when my hair comes out."

"It's hardly worth it," Ray replied with a deadpan expression.

From the beginning, I had accepted the news of breast cancer without the usual trauma. Two factors contributed to the sense of peace I experienced throughout each phase of the diagnosis and treatment. A few months earlier I had read a booklet that made a powerful case for healing, and the message stuck with me. As soon as I learned I might have a problem, I re-read the faith-building treatise. Any time my faith started to falter, I went back for a refresher course.

Another reason for my upbeat attitude had to do with a statement by my pastor. "Faith that hasn't been tested isn't really faith at all," he said. Hmm. My life had been quite carefree up to that point. Perhaps it was time for me to experience God's grace through adversity.

My surgery went extremely well. Operated on Wednesday, I went home on Thursday, and attended church on Sunday.

Before starting chemotherapy, I claimed God's promise in Jeremiah 29:11: *"I know the plans that I have for you," says the Lord, "plans for your welfare and not for harm, to give you a future with hope"* (NRSV). The verse told me that God would perform a chemical miracle. He would maximize the benefits of chemotherapy and minimize the harmful side effects.

With all I had going for me, I shouldn't have a problem at all with hair loss, right? After all, if I could handle losing a breast that wouldn't grow back, surely I could deal with a temporary loss of hair.

"Your hair will probably come out two weeks to the day from the first infusion," the nurse had told me.

When I woke up on the morning of the appointed day, my hair was intact. Would it survive a wash? I wondered. As I worked up a lather with the shampoo, the hair began to separate from my scalp. To avoid possibly shedding hair all over the house, I pulled it out by the handfuls. In moments it was gone, and I felt no particular emotion.

Then I looked in the mirror. I was a sorry sight. Looking more like a Martian than an earthling, I quickly donned a turban I had purchased for the occasion. My emotions took a downturn as the day progressed.

That evening I lamented the loss of my hair to my husband. For the first time in my battle with cancer, tears began to flow. To me, the turban didn't look much better than my bald head.

"I think you look cute in it," Ray said. When that didn't console me, he added, "I remember seeing Norma Shearer one time in a movie where she wore a turban. She looked pretty and so do you." Although I appreciated my husband's gallant effort, I still couldn't see it that way. I carried my pity-party to bed and didn't sleep well.

My sadness continued the following day. Thumbing through a magazine in the afternoon, an article caught my attention. In dealing with the aging process, the author had looked in the mirror and said, "What's so funny, Lord?"

The scene I pictured in my mind put a different spin on my situation. If God was laughing, why not laugh with Him? As I looked in the mirror with a smile and sparkling eyes, my self-esteem escalated. I took off the turban and discovered that even Martians look better with a happy face.

Before I started chemotherapy I had my hair cut short. At that time I started wearing a wig when I went out in public so people wouldn't notice a drastic change. Only a few close friends knew about my surgery and I wanted to keep it that way. The wig I purchased at a local salon pretty well matched my hair color and style. I didn't want to wear it all the time, though, because it was uncomfortable and hard to keep up.

Even with a positive attitude, I didn't enjoy wearing a turban or a scarf around the house. When I found a catalog showing wigs at a nominal cost, I decided to experiment. Measuring instructions indicated I needed a petite size, which turned out to be more comfortable. I ordered a short style in a blonde color about three shades lighter than my normal hair.

When I tried on the new wig and styled it, I felt like Cinderella — ready for the ball. "I know blondes have more fun," I told Ray, ""because I've been blonde for only an hour, and I'm having more fun already."

The next day I wore my new wig to the hospital for a shot. Looking at me with a question mark, the nurse said, "Bailey?"

""Do you notice anything different?" I asked.

"Yes. The wig. I like it."

The improvement of the new wig over the old one was so remarkable that I ordered two more of the new ones and scrapped the dowdy-looking one.

Compliments poured in from church friends who thought I had just changed hair color and style. I even received a telephone call from someone who had not been able to speak to me in person. My own hair had never caused that much of a sensation.

A couple of weeks later, an elderly man said to me, "I know you've had lots of comments on your hair, but I want to make one more. It's beautiful!"

I smiled and said, "Thank you." I'm sure God was smiling too.

Final Moments

Barbara Ragsdale

Shadows swirl around the veiled limbs;
The sun's slow arc tiptoes through the leaves.
An invisible movement turns night into day;
The unseen hand caresses the earth.

I am cold.

I press my cheek to yours;
Your warmth replaces my chill.
It's time to say goodbye;
I clutch your hand instead.

I am afraid.

You've asked, "What will it be like?"
I answer, "You will go to sleep."
A serene smile crosses your face;
You settle into silence.

I am numb.

Sun sparkles through the window;
I soothe your body with oil.
A fragrance to be remembered;
The scent will warm my thoughts.

I am sad.

I watch your breath, so slight;
It's barely able to move a feather.
The time is close;
I lean in to utter words that you cannot hear.

I am alone.

Silence fills the room, occupies all the space.
A heavy weight seals me in the chair.
Memories play in my mind.
The real has ceased; life is before and after.

You are at peace.

33

Three Little Words

Nanette Thorsen-Snipes

In 1981, my mother lay dying of lung cancer. She was raised in a different era, and neither she nor my military father showed me much affection while I was growing up — no hugs or kisses, and certainly no "I love you's," athough on some level, I felt they cared.

I recall being a nine-year-old in the 1950s and helping my mother feed our litter of German shepherd puppies when the mother dog became ill. Through this mothering process, I'd realized I was a born nurturer, because I not only fed but also cuddled and loved each of those s eleven quirming puppies. Even after their eyes opened, and they began their high-pitched barks, I'd named them all and played with them. And I'd cried when my mother sold them.

During those early years, I had wanted so much for Mama to embrace me and tell me she cared, but for whatever reason, she couldn't.

During the last two weeks of caregiving, as my mother lay in the hospital bed, a numbness engulfed me. I wanted to shout, "I love you, Mama!" But the words stuck to the roof of my mouth like a thick layer of peanut butter. How do you tell someone you love her when you haven't received an expression of love from her?

When I revisited the events in my life, thoughts of Mama flashed through my mind. Why hadn't she ever shown me affection? Why hadn't she ever hugged or kissed me? Didn't she love me? Those thoughts ate away at me.

One late afternoon, I brought a devotional to the hospital. I felt like a fraud reading about God since I had rarely been to church in those young adult years. But the devotional was all I had, and I clung to it, praying God would hear me and help me through my pain.

In the lengthening shadows of evening, I sat in the corner of Mama's room reading a devotion and praying God would show me how to say good-bye to my mother. The large hospital bed hid me from others' sight.

During this hushed and tranquil moment, a nurse in scrubs slipped into the room. I didn't know her but, in wonderment, I watched a scene play out before me.

I held my breath as the nurse stroked my mother's hair. Then, she bent forward and gently kissed Mama's cheek. Tears welled up in my eyes; that nurse did the one thing I could not. She showed my mother unconditional love. In His infinite mercy, for one moment in time, God held me close to His heart. He showed me how to love.

The next day, I watched Mama struggle to breathe. I thought I'd waited too long to say good-bye. Her brown eyes had an emotionless, glassy look from the pain medications. Recalling the scene from the night before, I touched her hand.

I looked at my frail mother, and in barely a whisper, I said, "I love you, Mama."

For a moment, my heart beat erratically — and time seemed to stand still.

Mama's eyes cleared and I whispered a thank you to the Lord. She looked directly at me, and for a brief moment in time my mother smiled at before disappearing again in a fog of pain.

I realize now that God's love is sufficient. *"My grace is sufficient for you, for my power is made perfect in weakness"* (2 Corinthians 12:9 NIV). That day, I was weak, but through His strength, I was finally able to express my love for my mother.

I thank Him every day for that kind nurse who showed me how to love my own mother.

34

Thank You for Finding My Breast Cancer

Melissa Henderson

What?
    Yes, you read the title correctly. Are you wondering why I would thank someone for finding my breast cancer?

In 2005, I visited the doctor and scheduled my routine yearly mammogram. My Mother had been diagnosed with breast cancer years before, so I knew the importance of regular screenings.

After I arrived on the scheduled day, images were taken and I was ready to go home to wait for results. There had been nothing out of the ordinary on my self-exam, so I had no cause for worry. The next day, however, a scheduler called to report I needed to return for more scans. The reason given was that the image machine was "acting up."

No worries. Just an inconvenience. I would return and have more images taken.

I entered the diagnostic center, checked in, found my spot on a comfy couch and reached for a magazine. While reading a story, I thought about others in the waiting room and wondered about their health concerns.

A technician called my name. I placed the magazine on the table in the center of the room, then followed this person into the image area. I went through the familiar procedure of taking my clothes off from the waist up and put on a hospital gown. Everything was the same as the first go round of images.

After the mammogram was completed, I sat in the waiting cubicle. A technician returned and asked me to follow her to another area. I became concerned. What was happening? After being told I needed more images, a nurse explained she would need to get the radiologist to speak with me. Then, I became anxious. This had not happened in the past.

The radiologist entered the room. I was lying on the exam table. Dim light filled the room as he showed the images to me. He explained each part of the breast and the areas of concern.

My breathing became quick and my heart pounded. How could this happen to me? Had I done something wrong with my body? I wanted answers. I began praying, *Lord, what should I do?*

Yes, there was a history of breast cancer but I truly never imagined it would hit our family again.

I was told to see my physician immediately. I dressed and walked to the parking lot where my husband was waiting for me. He had stayed in the car because we thought that visit would be a quick in-and-out trip. We had no idea there was an issue.

From that day forward, many appointments were made and kept. I chose my mother's surgeon and her radiologist. Daddy had been treated by the same radiologist for his lung cancer. Those doctors felt more like family than medical personnel.

Everything happened quickly that February in 2005, and beyond. From images to more images, to doctor visits to surgery, chemotherapy and radiation. Each moment was prayed for and appreciated.

During the course of treatments, my husband had an appointment at the diagnostic center. After his test, he noticed one of the radiologists behind the desk looking at charts.

"Excuse me," he said. "You are the radiologist who found my wife's breast cancer. We want to thank you." My husband spoke words that shocked the man.

"Pardon? What do you mean?" The radiologist explained that no one had ever thanked him for finding cancer.

"Sir, with your expertise, you found the tumor and my wife was able to get the diagnosis and help she needed immediately. We thank you for finding the lump and guiding her through the procedure."

The radiologist was touched by the words of my husband.

Yes, thanking someone for finding the tumor might sound strange. But we are thankful God gives wisdom and guidance to radiologists and other medical personnel so they can help us.

The next time you have a medical procedure, no matter the outcome, be sure to thank your doctors, nurses, volunteers and caregivers. Thank those people who are praying for you.

Once again, I will say to the radiologist, "Thank you for finding my breast cancer."

I am a seventeen-year breast cancer survivor. Praise be to God!

35

I Do

Andrea Merrell

The marriage vows were beautiful ... almost magical. I listened with heightened awareness as the bride and groom repeated the timeless words, "I do" and "I will." The young couple made promises to each other and created a covenant meant to last a lifetime.

As I heard the vows being made, I thought about how we enter our relationship with Jesus, our Bridegroom.

Jesus asked Peter, "Do you love Me?"

Peter's answer? "Of course I do, Lord."

Jesus asked men to follow Him as His disciples, and they said, "I will."

Jesus still asks questions of His followers today. *Do you trust Me? Will you serve Me? Will you forgive your brother? Will you be obedient to My Word?*

Too many of us make hasty vows when we need to be rescued from a bad situation: "God, if You'll get me out of this, I'll do anything you want me to do." Then, when He makes the slightest request — or doesn't respond the way we want — we can come up with a multitude of excuses and renege on our vow.

Making vain promises to God that we have no intention of keeping is not what He wants. His desire is for us to come to Him with a heart of love and adoration, giving ourselves completely to Him for all eternity. No strings attached. No fine print. No loopholes. And no backup plan.

In turn, we are given a husband, Father, Savior, protector, provider, comforter, healer, counselor, and a trusted friend. A covenant with our heavenly Bridegroom means everything we have is His, and everything He has is ours. All we have to do is believe and receive when we ask according to His Word.

The best news is that this covenant is not "until death do us part." In this relationship, when we cross death's threshold, that's when the real celebration begins.

If God is speaking to your heart today asking, *Do you love Me? Will you serve Me? . . .* let your answer be "Yes, Lord. I do and I will."

36

The Breath of Life

Yvonne Lehman

He is the God who made the world and everything in it....
He himself gives life and breath to everything....
For in him we live and move and exist.

Acts 17:24a, 25b, 28a NLT

2003

I got out of the shower, lifted my arms to wrap a towel around my wet hair, looked across into the mirror and noticed an indentation in my right breast. For an instant, my breath stopped. I'd heard that an indentation could mean an abnormal growth . . . or the dreaded word, *cancer*.

My first thoughts were that it shouldn't be anything more than a benign lump because my husband had been buried eleven months ago after a nine-month bout with cancer.

I was already scheduled for a mammogram (hadn't had one in four years — a mistake!). After the mammogram showed a "suspicious" spot, the doctor scheduled a biopsy for the following morning. A couple of days later I was told that I had infiltrating ductal carcinoma.

I taught my Sunday School class of senior citizens and told them I had breast cancer. Many of them related their own stories of having had the cancer or knowing those who had. One person said, "We ask 'Why me?' don't we?"

Without hesitation, I answered from the depth of my soul. "No, I don't ask 'Why me?' I have no more right to be well than anyone else."

At that moment, I began to realize how I felt about having cancer. I was not in denial but in the early stages of acceptance, alive, feeling well, and saw no reason to act like I'd received a death sentence. I had a disease that might be healed, might cause me to suffer, might kill me.

I have no control over whether I will breathe one more breath of life. Admitting my inability to control my life brings me closer to the creator, the sustainer, the omniscient, omnipotent God.

Breathing and living become an act of worship, of realizing what is most important in life . . . and it's not my personal success, my bank account, or the size of my house. It is my relationship with my Lord and Savior, Jesus Christ.

After my surgery, I was told that my cancer was ER/PR positive and they were waiting for the HER2/neu test. The Bible tells us in 1 Thessalonians 5:18 to *give thanks in all circumstances, for this is God's will for you in Christ Jesus.*

Could I give thanks for cancer?

Yes, but could I mean it?

I want to have perfect health — a perfect life. However, we are not living in a perfect world. The Bible tells us there is an appointed time for each of us to die, and I try to accept that. However, I love life. I love God's beautiful creation. I love my freedom to go, do, enjoy and become. I love my family. I love my failures and difficulties that have brought me closer to God and taught me what life's priorities should be.

And yes, I have prayed for healing.

I realize that "dying" is a form of healing if we have accepted Jesus into our hearts and lives. My prayers are not exclusively the "give me" kind of prayers. They include a "make me, heal me, use me, take me" kind of prayers.

The HER/2neu test came back negative, which is good. However, neither the doctors nor I know if cancer is lurking in there or if it will show up again — just as we don't know if I'll make it to the Post Office one more time in my car.

But as Dr. Hetzel said, "If the cancer returns, we'll deal with it." That's the doctor who got on his knees before my surgery, held my hands and prayed to God. There's no doubt that God is in this. He knows my purpose. He knows his plans for me. And he knows when it's time to call me home.

I don't know that my attitude would be as accepting if I were a young mother with children to raise. I only know that I have been greatly blessed, and I have positive proof of God's workings in my life, so I cannot complain.

There is one thing I intend to remember, and that's the saying, "Life is not measured by the number of breaths we take, but by the moments that take our breath away."

* * *

2020

The above was written a couple of months after the cancer, in 2003. In keeping with that saying, I began making plans to go the place that was the desire of my heart — Israel. When I talked about it, many people said they would be afraid to go there because of the physical danger. My response was that my husband died of cancer at home. As long as I can choose, I will choose taking the risks of personal danger. Just as I take Femara — a pill for cancer — daily I will take precautions, but I will not allow fear to keep me from enjoying the wonderful things in life. I'd rather die in a plane crash, or a bomb in Israel, than while sitting "safely" at home.

My pastor/son and fun/daughter agreed with me, so the three of us went together with a tour to Israel in 2004. We each found this the trip of a lifetime that we would not have wanted to miss. It was like walking in the pages of the Bible. I was privileged to see my son standing where Jesus stood 2,000 years ago, reading and commenting on the Beatitudes. I rode in a boat on the Sea of Galilee and felt so close to God I understood how Peter could have thought, for a few moments, that he could walk on water as Jesus did.

I stood in the Garden of Gethsemane where Jesus sweat drops of blood and cried out, "Not my will, but Thine." I saw Mount Calvary where Jesus was crucified, and a tomb like the one from which He arose. I prayed at the Wailing Wall, cried in high priest's courtyard where Peter denied Jesus three times. I saw and understood where the final battle, Armageddon, will take place.

Impressed upon me was that we don't have to fight our battles alone. The Holy Spirit is available to us, and it's so true that this life is but a breath compared with eternity. Our opportunities and pleasures vanish as quickly as grass withers.

My family used to say, "Oh, you and dad will outlive us all." I think this was just a way of not wanting to fully face the fact of death. After his death I'd say, "Your dad didn't outlive you, and I probably won't either."

I think my having had breast cancer impressed upon us the reality of death.

When families face the reality of death, there comes a better appreciation of the living. When we admit we won't be on this earth forever, we can appreciate the wonders and beauty of this earth. My daughter exemplified that the summer of 2006 when she, her husband, and eight-year-old son took me along to Paris with them. I'd always wanted to go, and she realized this might be the last opportunity we had to do that together.

For three years, I didn't care that my right breast was missing. I was simply grateful that I had survived the cancer for that length of time. But I began to miss having the body of a woman and I opted for reconstruction. The surgeon did a fantastic job and I told him I hadn't looked so good since I was young and pregnant. However, I knew that what's beneath the skin is artificial, not really flesh and blood, but a soft packet of saline solution. My body only looks and feels like the real thing.

Therein is a lesson. A person can look whole and complete, but we do not know what their skin is really covering. Perhaps it's a bout with cancer or some other pain, whether it's mental, emotional, physical, or spiritual lack. I want my life not just to be what it looks like on the outside, the complete figure, the smile, the clothing. I want my life to mean something to the world, not just be a shell with skin on it.

We don't always know what is going on in our bodies, what may suddenly become apparent, like the day in 2003 when I looked in the mirror and knew something wasn't right. Of course, I've known other times when things weren't "right" in my physical, mental, emotional, spiritual self. That brush with possible death made me more determined to be all I can be, do what I can do, not play around with life but use it effectively.

Facing death has given me a greater desire to love life.

I remember, when I was a little girl, I asked my grandmother what life was like for her, being old. She said, "Why honey, life is just as precious to me as it was when I was your age."

I now know what she meant. I love this life, but having faced and gone through a disease that could have taken my life, I appreciate life even more than I ever have.

I came away with this new determination: I will not just exist, but until I die . . . I will live life to its fullest.

Publisher's Note: We lost Yvonne in the late spring of 2021, not to cancer or even Covid. Her body just couldn't recover completely after suffering a stroke several months earlier. But until her death at age 82, Yvonne Lehman lived and loved life to the fullest . . . and that zest for life impacted thousands of others.

About the Authors

Ozlem Buber Barnard is a woman of faith, military spouse of 21 years, mother of three (two teenagers and a toddler, oh my!), mentor, and a fierce protector of justice.

She is the author of several published articles relating to the hardships military families go through during deployments and their frequent moves.

Ozlem works full time as an attorney in gloomy Washington D.C., but dreams about a future where she can live in a sunny beach location and write encouraging stories full time. Her goal in life is to be the best version of herself that God created her to be and to lead by example.

Bob Blundell is a freelance writer and converted Catholic. His work has been published in magazines such as *America, Liguorian, The Bible Advocate*, and *Crosscurrents*. He has also had essays published in several of the *Divine Moments* series. A winner of the 2021 Christian Writers Award, he is scheduled to release his first solo book, *Crossroads* in 2023. He and his wife Dee live in the Houston area.

Ginny Dent Brant is a speaker and writer who grew up in the halls of power in Washington, D.C. She has battled cancer, ministered around the world, and served as a counselor, educator, wellness advocate, and adjunct professor.

Her award-winning book, *Finding True Freedom: From the White House to the World*, was endorsed by Chuck Colson and featured in many TV and media interviews. Her recent book, *Unleash Your God-given Healing: Eight Steps to Prevent and Survive Cancer* was written with commentary from an oncologist and medical researcher, Dr. Robert Elliott. It has received five awards including a Golden Scrolls and a Selah Award and has been featured on *CBN, CTN, Atlanta Live*, etc. Learn more about cancer prevention and wellness on her blog: www.ginnybrant.com.

Rob Buck has been married to Betsy for 40 years. They have four children and seven grandchildren. He is president of an IT training company and on the board of directors of Focused Living Ministries. He's an Elder at Columbia Crossroads church and a member of Word Weavers International. Rob has published two novels and is a blogger (www.joy-in-the-journey.com). He's also a chicken farmer who has a 21-hole disc golf course in his back yard.

Steve Carter has lived exclusively in the South. A Bible College graduate, he has spent the majority of his life in service to The Risen Christ. Currently, his primary ministry is safeguarding congregations by training and participating in armed security teams. A physical fitness enthusiast, he has participated in numerous running and bicycling sports, with the most noteworthy being peddling across the Continental United States twice. He spends his leisure time enjoying his grandchildren and playing drums.

Janet Ann Collins has been a writer and teacher. She worked at California School for the Deaf for many years. She and her husband raised three deaf foster children in addition to their birth daughter. She is currently retired and lives in the lovely Sierra Nevada foothills of California. She loves to read and is pleased to be able to do so with both eyes.

Ben Cooper is a Christian, husband, father, writer, speaker, beekeeper, and more. He is a double cancer survivor, and used his second diagnosis to begin writing. Growing up on a family farm, getting an Ag degree from Penn State University, working 32 years for Maryland Department of Agriculture, and being a beekeeper has allowed him to spend much of his time around animals and nature. He uses that as the basis for writing his books and writing for Guideposts' *All God's Creatures* and their newest devotional titled *Inspiration from the Garden*. He resides in the foot slopes of the eastern Continental Divide in southern Pennsylvania. You can contact him at cooperville@breezeline.net

Lola Di Giulio De Maci is a retired teacher whose stories have appeared in numerous editions of *Chicken Soup for the Soul, Los Angeles Times, Reminisce, Divine Moments*, newspapers, and children's publications. Lola has a Master of Arts in education and English. She writes overlooking the San Bernardino Mountains.

Diana C. Derringer is an award-winning writer and author of *Beyond Bethlehem and Calvary: 12 Dramas for Christmas, Easter, and More*! Her articles, devotions, dramas, planning guides, Bible studies, and poems have been accepted more than 1,000 times in over 70 publications, including *The Upper Room, The Secret Place, Clubhouse, Kentucky Monthly, Country,* and *Missions Mosaic,* plus several anthologies. She also writes radio drama for Christ to the World Ministries and shares weekly blog posts on *Words, Wit, and Wisdom: Life Lessons from English Expressions.* Her adventures as a social worker, adjunct professor, youth Bible study teacher, and friendship family for international university students supply a constant flow of writing ideas. Visit her at dianaderringer.com. You can also find her on Facebook, Twitter, LinkedIn, Instagram, Goodreads, Pinterest, and her Amazon page.

Tanja Dufrene's seemingly chance encounter at a local crafter's mall awakened her childhood desire to communicate through writing. While leading a ladies group at her local church, she recognized the sincerity of many Christ followers, but concerned about their lack of Biblical knowledge she began to write a weekly devotional hoping to inspire her readers to draw closer to God through simply reading His Word. Some of those writings are found in *Artesian Zeal*, her first devotional book. Another ladies' Bible study resulted in the *Warrior of the Word* Bible study series. Both are available through Amazon and Barnes & Noble. Tanja became an ordained minister in 2011. She shares a daily minute devotional on her Warrior of the Word Facebook page. Follow her on Twitter, Instagram and Pintrest. Contact her at WarrioftheWord@yahoo.com.

Mindy Gallagher writes personal interest stories, and blogs. In addition, she is a singer/songwriter and professional worship leader on staff at Bellview Baptist Church in Woodruff, South Carolina. She is currently working on her memoir, a portion of which, "The Field," can be found in *Pandemic Moments: Stories of the 2020 COVID-19 Outbreak*. Mindy and her husband, Jim, reside in Greer, South Carolina with their chihuahua, Sophie, spaniel mutt, Charlie, and black cat, Johnny. Their two grown daughters reside in the frozen tundra of Minnesota, from which she and her husband escaped for early retirement in 2018.

Deborah Gatz, married to her husband of 39 years, is the mother of four grown children and grandmother of five amazing grandchildren. Active in her local church, she has assisted with teaching or leading women's Bible studies. Her main desire is to see people come to know Jesus or to grow in their relationship with Christ. An avid reader, Deb has written for several years. It is her hope and prayer that her story will encourage readers going through life's trials. Her cancer journey continues with five recurrences since the initial diagnosis, yet her experience is that God remains faithful and present no matter what life throws at her.

Lydia E. Harris has been married to her college sweetheart, Milt, for more than 55 years. She enjoys spending time with her family, which includes two married children and five grandchildren ages 12 to 23. She is the author of two books for grandparents: *Preparing My Heart for Grandparenting: for Grandparents at Any Stage of the Journey* and *In the Kitchen with Grandma: Stirring Up Tasty Memories Together*. With a master's degree in Home Economics, Lydia creates and tests recipes with her grandchildren for Focus on the Family children's magazines. She also pens the column "A Cup of Tea with Lydia," which is published in the US and Canada. It's no wonder she is known as "Grandma Tea."

Melissa Henderson, an award-winning author, writes inspirational messages sometimes laced with a bit of humor. Melissa hopes to encourage readers with her articles, devotions, and stories online and in print publications. She is the author of *Licky the Lizard* and *Grumpy the Gator*.

Melissa's passions are helping in community and church. She is an Elder, Deacon and Stephen Minister. Follow her on Facebook, Twitter, Pinterest and at melissaghenderson.com.

Beckie Horter writes from her home in the hills of western Pennsylvania.

After graduating from Geneva College, she set out to report on the news of man, working at the local newspaper. Vision loss quickly changed her plans.

In what turned out to be a divine interruption, God used blindness to grab Beckie's attention and focus her gaze on Him. Her writing dreams revived and she began telling people about the Good News of Jesus, the most important story ever.

Beckie is a frequent contributor to *Light Magazine* as well as a blog writer and peer advisor for The American Printing House for the Blind.

She enjoys walking, biking, listening to the birds, and spending time with her two goldendoodles.

Yvonne Lehman, award-winning, best-selling author of over 75 books — including 59 novels — with more than 3 million books in print, has been published throughout the US and in Germany, Holland, and Norway. Her genres include Romance, Women's Fiction, Christian Fiction, Cozy Mystery, Young Adult, biblical times and stories including suspense, humor, true events and thought-provoking plots with intriguing characters.

Yvonne earned a Master's Degree in English Literature from Western Carolina University and taught English and Creative Writing on the college level.

She founded and for 25 years directed the Blue Ridge Mountains Christian Writers Conference, held at the Ridgecrest North Carolina Conference Center. After turning that over to another leader, she founded and directed the Blue Ridge "Autumn in the Mountains" Novelist Retreat for 12 years.

Until her death in May 2021, Yvonne compiled and edited the Grace Publishing House *Divine Moments* anthologies. *Moments with Billy Graham* was a 2019 Selah Finalist. *Christmas Stories* was a Selah finalist in 2021.

Jeri McBryde loves sharing her life experiences with the hope of helping others. Her stories have appeared in nine *Chicken Soup for the Soul* books. She has been published in the *Divine Moments* anthology *Remembering Christmas*. Her works also appear in three other anthologies. Jeri lives in a small southern delta town. Retired, she spends her days reading and working on her dream of publishing a novel. A doting grandmother, her world revolves around faith, family, friends, and chocolate.

Diana Leagh Matthews is a vocalist, speaker, writer, life coach, and genealogist. During the day, she is a certified Activities Director for a skilled nursing facility. She is a monthly contributor to *Ruby Magazine* and has been published on a variety of websites and anthologies, including many books in the Divine Moments series. She currently resides in South Carolina. Visit her at www.DianaLeaghMatthews.com and www.alookthrutime.com.

Andrea Merrell is an associate editor with Christian Devotions Ministries and Lighthouse Publishing of the Carolinas. She is also a professional freelance editor and was a finalist for the 2016 Editor of the Year Award at BRMCWC. She teaches workshops at writers conferences and has been published in numerous anthologies and online venues. Andrea is a graduate of Christian Communicators and a finalist in the 2015 USA Best Book Awards. She is the author of *Murder of a Manuscript* and *Praying for the Prodigal*. Her newest book, *Marriage: Make It or Break It*, is available on Amazon. For more information visit www.AndreaMerrell.com or www.TheWriteEditing.com.

Norma C. Mezoe has been a published writer for 37 years. Her writing has appeared in books, devotionals, Sunday school take-home papers, and magazines. She is active in her church in a variety of roles. Norma became a Christian at the age of 15, but didn't grow spiritually in a significant way until a crisis at the age of 33 brought her into a closer relationship with the Lord. Norma may be contacted at: normacm@tds.net.

Brenda Miller, a survivor of the losses of loved ones due to the ravage of cancer, was born into a Christian farm family in Kentucky. She graduated high school and attended college, then married a hometown boy. Four children were born to this union and raised with past generational values. She writes about life as a Christian wife, mother, grandmother, and caregiver. She has published two books, *God's Unfailing Love* and *Set Your House in Order . . . Reflections on God's Divine Order*, and contributed to other published works. She continues to write from her family farmhouse, posting weekly on Restorations Church's Facebook page. She is blessed with thirteen grandchildren, three great-grandchildren.

Maureen Miller, wife, mother of three, and "Mora" to two, lives on Selah Farm, a hobby homestead nestled in the mountains of western North Carolina. With a passion for God's Word, she writes regularly for a number of online devotion sites and compilation devotionals, as well as for her local newspaper. Praying to have eyes and ears open that she might experience God in the miracles of His created world, she blogs about such at www.penningpansies.com. Her debut novel is under contract with Redemption Press.

Vicki H. Moss is a former pundit for the *American Daily Herald* and former Editor-at-Large and Contributing Editor for *Southern Writers Magazine*. She's written over 750 articles and taught writing workshops throughout the South. Her books include *Writing with Voice, How to Write for Kids Magazines, Adrift, Rogue Hearts, Nailed It!,* and *Smelling Stinkweed*. With a writing project always in the works, Vicki does find time to grow and snip a few dahlias, roses, peonies, and camellias while teaching grandies how to garden and write poetry.

April Pope and her husband. JW. live and work on their farm that borders Cape Fear River in central North Carolina. While JW mainly tends the cattle, April is shepherdess to a flock of sheep who serve as her inspiration for weekly devotions called "pasture parables." Off the farm, her life as a family medicine PA and Campbell University faculty member keeps her busy, but when time allows, April loves to saddle up a horse and ride the trails that traverse their 600-acre property. She loves photographing their farm life, working with livestock guardian dogs, and cooking. Check out the Cape Fear FarmLife Facebook and Instagram pages to read weekly pasture parables. Visit Capefearfarmlife.com for Blog posts about her life on the farm.

Debbie Presnell, member of Gardner-Webb University's Gallery of Distinguished Alumni, is a published author, national speaker, Bible study teacher, and the United States spokesperson for Mukti Mission in India. In addition to several articles in the *Divine Moments* series, she has published a devotional book, and several Bible studies, all available on Amazon.

Debbie is founder and director of *Shine Camp* — whose mission is equipping middle and high school girls with Biblical principles to embrace their identity in Christ and discover their purpose. She brings devotions and inspirational messages on YouTube and Facebook @ ShineEveryDayWithDebbie, and blogs at debbiepresnell.com/blog/. Visit her website: debbiepresnell.com

Debbie loves both the mountains and the beach, hiking, biking, and spending time with her family — especially coffee time and shopping with her girls. Email her at debbie@debbiepresnell.com.

Barbara Ragsdale is an award-winning short story writer. Her stories are published in three *Chicken Soup for the Soul* anthologies as well as multiple sort-story collections published by CC Writers. Her story "A Walking Miracle" is published in Guidepost's *Miracles Do Happen.*

Her awards include recognition from Southwest Writers and National Pen Women in non-fiction story competitions. Her poem "How Will He Know He Is Beautiful?" was published by an ezine. She was a columnist and staff writer for *Southern Writers Magazine.*

She was editor and publisher for a newsletter for the League of Women Voters, has written devotionals, a Lenten series, and interviews for a church newsletter.

When not writing, she is an exercise instructor with the Silver Sneakers program.

Marian Rizzo, Pulitzer Prize nominee in journalism, has won numerous writing awards, including the New York Times Chairman's Award and first place in the 2014 Amy Foundation Writing Awards. She worked for the *Ocala Star-Banner* newspaper for 30 years and has written articles for the *Ocala Gazette*, *Ocala Style Magazine*, and *Decision Magazine.*

In 2018, her suspense novel, *Muldovah*, was a finalist in the Genesis competition at the ACFW Conference.

Marian earned a bachelor's degree in Bible education. She trained for jungle missions with New Tribes (now ETHNOS 360), and served at a Youth With A Mission training center in Southern Spain.

Marian lives in Florida with her daughter, Vicki, who has Down Syndrome. Her other daughter, Joanna, has blessed her with three wonderful grandchildren.

Nanette Thorsen-Snipes is a freelance editor, proofreader, and writer in the Christian publishing industry. She has contributed stories/devotions to more than 60 books (Guideposts *Miracle* series, *Chicken Soup for the Soul*, *New Women's Devotional Bible*, *Grace Givers*, among others), and she has written numerous magazine articles, devotions, and children's stories. Her most recent stories are in *Broken Moments* and *Christmas Stories,* previous books in the *Divine Moments* series. In October, *Christmas Cats,* edited by Lonnie Hull DuPont, Revell Books, will be published. Contact Nanette at nsnipes@bellsouth.net.

Erma Ullrey, married for 40 years, enjoys four wonderful children, three outlaws, and four precious grandchildren. She worked in the medical field for over 25 years, becoming a health educator with international credentials.

A women's Bible study leader, she also participates in a local book club, and local and national writers groups. She posts encouraging blogs on her website each Friday, and enjoys chatting with Facebook, Twitter, and Instagram friends.

Erma's recent awards include 2022 ACFW Genesis semi-finalist, ACFW 2020 First Impressions 1st place; 2020 ICAN 2nd place; 2020 ACFW Virginia Crown Award 1st place.

Her picture book *A Snowflake's Adventure* was published in October 2021 under the pseudonym eMarie. For each book sold, she donates another to Operation Christmas Child.

Learn more at https://www.merryheartink.com.

Beverly Varnado, an award-winning author and screenwriter, is also a blogger and artist. She writes both non-fiction and fiction. Her most recent book, the Christmas novella *A Season for Everything,* is a sequel to her novels *A Plan for Everything* and *The Key to Everything.* Her blog, *One Ringing Bell,* has nearly 1,000 posts in its archives. Beverly's work has been featured on World Radio, in the *Upper Room Magazine,* and in several periodicals, anthologies, and online sites. She has been a finalist for the prestigious Kairos Prize in screenwriting.

Always working on a new painting, Beverly enjoys participating in gallery exhibits. She lives in north Georgia with her husband, Jerry, is Mom to three, and Mimi to two. Learn more at www. Beverly Varnado.com.

Ann Brubaker Greenleaf Wirtz, an award-winning author, received the Willie Parker Peace History Book Award from the North Carolina Society of Historians for *The Henderson County Curb Market.* She has written *Sorrow Answered, Hand of Mercy,* and numerous articles for her local newspaper. Every December, her nostalgic remembrance of Christmas in the 1950s and '60s in her hometown of Webster Groves, Missouri, is published in *The Pulse*. She has stories in *Chicken Soup for the Soul, More Christmas Moments, Loving Moments, Cool-inary Moments, Moments with Billy Graham* and *Grandma's Cookie Jar*. Ann is the mother of one very dear son and daughter-in-law, and the grandmother of two adored grandchildren. She and her beloved husband, Patrick, reside in Hendersonville, North Carolina.

Divine Moments

If you want to read more faith-filled stories like those in *Can, Sir!*, you'll love the other books in this series, available through your favorite online retailer or on our website: grace-publishing.com.

Divine Moments ~ God's Amazing Presence in Our Lives
Christmas Moments ~ The True Meaning of Christmas
Spoken Moments ~ The Power of Words
Precious, Precocious Moments ~ Children, Childhood, and Faith
More Christmas Moments ~ The Wonders of Christmas
Stupid Moments ~ Those Sensitive Times and What We Learn From Them
Additional Christmas Moments ~ Celebrating the True Spirit of Christmas
Why? Titanic Moments ~ Stories and Photos Offering a Glimpse into the Enduring Significance of the Ship and Its Passengers
Loving Moments ~ The Many Faces of Love
Merry Christmas Moments ~ The Wonder of Christmas
Cool-inary Moments ~ Memories, Mishaps, Masterpieces, and Recipes Flavored with a Little Advice
Moments with Billy Graham ~ Personal Recollections of America's Beloved Evangelist
Personal Titanic Moments ~ Life-Changing Sink-or-Swim Decisions
Remembering Christmas ~ Recalling the Joys and Cherished Memories of Simpler Times
Romantic Moments ~ Those Special Feelings, Relationships, and True Love
Pandemic Moments ~ Stories of the 2020 Covid-19 Outbreak
Christmas Stories ~ Celebrating Christmas with Family Traditions
Broken Moments ~ How Transformation Is Possible With Christ
Celebrating Christmas ~ Sharing God's Perfect Gift
Grandma's Cookie Jar ~ Special Times, Memories, and Recipes

www.ingramcontent.com/pod-product-compliance
Lightning Source LLC
LaVergne TN
LVHW051500070426
835507LV00022B/2853